Association for
Supervision and
Curriculum Development

Moving Toward
Self-Directed
Learning

Highlights of Relevant
Research and of
Promising Practices

Delmo Della-Dora
and
Lois Jerry Blanchard, editors

Contributors:

James J. Berry • Lois Jerry Blanchard
Arthur L. Costa • Delmo Della-Dora
Benjamin P. Ebersole • Mario D. Fantini
Richard L. Foster • Anthony Gregorc
Claire B. Halverson • Patricia Knudsen
Alberto Ochoa • James V. Orr
Ana Maria Rodriguez • Barbara A. Sizemore
Nancy Spencer • James D. Wells
Edwin White

ASCD

225 North Washington Street
Alexandria, Virginia 22314

Stock number: 611-79166

Library of Congress Catalog Card Number: 79-64506

ISBN 0-87120-094-5

Contents

Foreword / iv
Benjamin P. Ebersole

Preface / v
Delmo Della-Dora

1. **What Is Self-Directed Learning? / 1**

2. **Promising Practices and Relevant Research / 11**

3. **Needed Research and Educational Development Work / 39**

4. **Social-Cultural Forces Affecting Self-Directed Learning / 49**

   Forces Which Affect Self-Direction and Self-Responsibility of
   Students • Barbara A. Sizemore / 50

   Individual and Cultural Determinants of Self-Directed Learning Ability:
   Straddling an Instructional Dilemma • Claire Halverson / 53

   Forces Which Affect Self-Direction and Self-Responsibility of
   Students • Alberto M. Ochoa and Ana Maria Rodriguez / 65

5. **Developing Self-Directed Learning Programs / 77**
   Lois Jerry Blanchard

Contributors / 95

Foreword

Premises:

- That most people live in a world largely created by themselves
- That most people do those things most effectively which make sense to them
- That for complete living people need to make choices about and be responsible for their own behavior.

The premises on which this book is based are consistent with the ASCD purpose of furthering self-respect, self-discipline, and self-responsibility. The authors cast these premises in the context of our culture, with balance between societal rules and conditions on the one hand and individual rights and responsibilities on the other.

They make the point that all of us, the teachers and the taught, need to be moving toward self-direction. This does not mean leading unstructured, calloused lives. Quite the opposite. It means knowing more about who we are, where we are going, and how to get there in a caring and disciplined manner. It means we need to work for the creation of those conditions which make fulfilled lives an increasing possibility for every individual. It means taking responsibility for our own lives because only to the extent that this is done do we grow and become educated human beings.

With its definitions, review of literature, examples of current practices, practical suggestions, and encouragement to explore, this publication will be a source of information for those who want to know more about self-directed learning, and a reservoir of ideas and inspiration to those dedicated to the furtherance of these efforts.

BENJAMIN P. EBERSOLE
President, 1979-80
Association for Supervision and
Curriculum Development

Preface

Each person needs to learn to plan, to make wise choices, and to take responsibility for his/her life. Survival of our society, as a whole, requires that we learn how to plan wisely together. Moreover, it is clear that individually and collectively we need to improve in our ability to be self-directing and self-responsible—and to have continuing faith in our ability to do so—if democracy itself is to survive.

Schooling in America periodically gives explicit major attention to the knowledge, values, and skills needed by citizens in a democratic society. These cycles in education alternate with cycles in which the focus of schooling is on "back to the basics." The "basics" in this context refer primarily to the skills of reading, writing, and arithmetic, of course. The "basics" needed for survival of, and improvement in, democratic practices include the "3 R's" and much more. It is that expanded view of the "basics" with which this publication is concerned, and to which the ASCD Project on Self-Directed Learning has given its attention during its first year of existence.

ASCD's Project on Self-Directed Learning was initiated in October of 1977. Its members (Lois Jerry Blanchard, Delmo Della-Dora, Richard Foster, and Anthony Gregorc) outlined a publication which would be the first step in a series of proposed actions designed to encourage and assist in further development of school programs fostering self-directed learning.

This publication is intended to be a reference source for people interested in fostering self-directed learning. It describes the characteristics of self-directed learners and also attempts to summarize the highlights of promising practices and relevant research of the past 50 years. Many programs initiated in past years were effective in dealing with some aspect of self-directed learning but were not widely disseminated and few people now recall them. A great deal of research which is relevant to this issue has been reported in past years to the small audience who reads research findings. Relatively little has been applied in schools. It is hoped that this publication will call attention to these practices and research so that they will be used more widely. Another aim is to stimulate more research in areas which will improve the state of the art.

Not enough attention has been given to the impact of social and cultural forces on teaching and learning—certainly not to the ways in which such forces affect the development of self-directed learning. Chapter 4 attempts to do so, based on research and practices reported by four experienced practitioners.

Finally, in Chapter 5, there is a description of ways of initiating and fostering self-directed learning in a school, district, college, or other institution.

The draft outline for the publication was developed by Lois Jerry Blanchard, Delmo Della-Dora, Richard Foster, and Anthony Gregorc. It was reviewed by a number of individuals, by those attending an open meeting at the ASCD Annual Conference in San Francisco in March 1978, and by Unit Presidents of ASCD in May 1978. Excellent ideas were received for content and for potential contributors from these sources.

Delmo Della-Dora drafted Chapters 1, 2, and 3 and incorporated in them contributions from Nancy Spencer and Edwin White (Chapter 1) and Anthony Gregorc, James Wells, Pat Knudsen, James Orr, and James Berry (Chapter 2).

Chapter 4 was written by Barbara Sizemore, Claire Halverson, Alberto Ochoa, and Ana Maria Rodriguez, and edited by Delmo Della-Dora.

Chapter 5 was drafted and edited by Lois Jerry Blanchard with contributions from Arthur L. Costa, Delmo Della-Dora, Mario Fantini, and Richard Foster, and helpful suggestions from Robert Anderson (Texas Tech University), Robert S. Gilchrist (U.S. International University, San Diego), and H. Vaughn Phelps (Westside Community Schools, Omaha).

Project members Foster, Blanchard, and Gregorc provided constructive comments on drafts of all chapters as did William C. Miller (Wayne County Intermediate School District, Michigan), David Thatcher (Sonoma State College, California), Edwin White (State Department of Education, Virginia), Judith Hunt and June Gifford (both of California State University at Hayward). A graduate student, Judy Krupp, assisted Tony Gregorc in gathering research findings on learning styles for Chapter 2.

The members of the Project on Self-Directed Learning thank all those who assisted in the preparation of material for publication.

DELMO DELLA-DORA
Project Director

1.
What Is
Self-Directed Learning?

Self-directed learning refers to characteristics of schooling which should distinguish education in a democratic society from schooling in autocratic societies. In a democratic society, students need to have opportunities to learn how to choose *what* is to be learned, *how* it is to be learned, *when* it is to be learned, and *how to evaluate* their own progress. Students need to learn all this in settings which provide for the active assistance and cooperation of teachers and other adults, and of their peers.

The question of what ages or stages of development are appropriate for learning these skills is a critical one because many parents and school people are not convinced that students are capable of learning decision-making skills and of assuming the consequent responsibilities until they are of high school or even of college age.

However, the authors of this publication are convinced that young people are capable of beginning to learn to participate in significant ways in educational decision making in the elementary school. By the time they are entering early adolescence, most young people are capable of participating in major ways in determining educational goals, subject matter for learning, methods for learning/teaching, and ways of assessing educational achievement. Support for this belief is found in a number of school practices throughout the country as well as in a substantial body of related research. The relevant practices and research span a period of some 30 to 50 years but are not yet widely known even among professional educators. A brief summary of the highlights of these school programs and of the relevant research is contained in Chapter 2.

Self-directed learning is *not* synonymous with what is generally referred to as individualized instruction. Current approaches to individualized instruction often involve having teachers learn how to: (1) diagnose pupil learning needs, (2) prescribe educational activities to fit the diagnosis, and (3)

1

monitor progress to assure that the prescription is being followed and to validate the diagnosis. The language of these approaches is borrowed from the medical profession, the educational psychology is behavioristic in conceptualization, and the inherent philosophy is essentially authoritarian in character. Such approaches to individualizing instruction provide little or no opportunity for students to learn either the skills of decision making or to learn to take on any responsibility for their own learning.

The roles of the teacher in self-directed learning are vital ones but their nature varies in many ways from those which are prevalent for most teachers today. Certain functions remain essentially the same, however. One example of similarity is that the teacher should be an active participant with individual students and with the class group in all aspects of the learning process, whether it be in a completely teacher-directed setting or one in which students are learning to be self-directed and self-responsible.

Another teacher role which should be in evidence with all teaching styles is to make clear that being self-directed in a democratic society includes being sensitive to the delicate balance between societal rules on one hand and individual rights and responsibilities on the other. This balance requires continuous attention from teacher and students. In this connection, it is important for students to learn that decision making operates within prescribed limits. Teachers need to help students discover what the current limits of decision making are in every school situation and must indicate the source of the constraints (law, board policies, school regulations, teacher opinion). This does not imply that the limits, once discovered, are to be accepted unquestioningly but only that they should be known, as part of the information necessary for decision making. Ways of producing desired change in the current rules, opinions, regulations, policies, and laws must also be given major emphasis.

These similarities in the role of the teacher in traditional teaching and in teaching for self-directed learning are noted because to some educators the phrase *self*-directed may connote that teachers become less important. Others may be concerned that self-directed means "selfish-directed" and that it may foster self-indulgent qualities in students. Neither of these inferences is correct, as will be illustrated in the subsequent material.

This is an excellent period in our history for review of educational efforts which involve students in making decisions about their own learning. Among the reasons for doing so:

1. *Awareness of Non-traditional Approaches.* Many (perhaps most) educators, parents, and students today are familiar only with teacher-directed and school-prescribed practices for teaching and learning.

This generalization may not be true for a large number of active members of the Association for Supervision and Curriculum Development or for experienced educational innovators. But, the general public and a large proportion of educators do not know that there is both a body of useful educational research and a 50 year history of successful programs and practices which support the basic principles of self-directed learning.

Everyone involved with education of people in the elementary and secondary schools should at least be aware of this kind of research and of the relevant promising practices as they make decisions about whether to move toward more teacher-direction or toward more self-direction by students in planning school programs.

2. *Reference Source for Support of Self-Directed Learning.* In those cases where self-directed learning programs are underway, or are being considered, it would be of value to be able to refer to the supporting data for such programs. This could be used either to renew one's own faith or in discussions with potential supporters.

3. *Mutual Support Systems.* A number of people are interested in the kinds of learning advocated in this publication. However, many of them feel alone in their interests and/or efforts because popular opinion inside and outside the profession is heading in another direction. The members of the ASCD Project on Self-Directed Learning intend to facilitate communication between individuals and groups interested in the many kinds of self-directed learning programs by assisting in the establishment of networks of people who wish to support each other's activities. This publication is viewed as only one activity in a series which both the national Association for Supervision and Curriculum Development and various ASCD state units will undertake to foster the movement toward self-directed learning.

4. *Relationships Among Varied Approaches.* Each education movement, old or new, attracts a band of faithful adherents. Often, they become so involved in proposing and in defending their own particular program that there is not enough energy left over to explore common elements and relationships with other similar programs and practices. The authors believe this is true in the case of self-directed learning programs and will attempt to indicate areas of overlapping interest and common goals among many different programs.

5. *Bases for Developing New Programs.* People who are dissatisfied with attempts to carry out competency-based education, and with the narrowly-defined and prescriptive sets of grade-level standards for graduation now springing up all over the country, will find it helpful to consider alternatives.

6. *Available Research and Promising Practices.* As noted earlier, the awareness of useful research and of promising practices is severely limited in education. Some reasons for this are discussed in Chapter 3. This phenomenon also exists in other fields; it is not unique to our profession.

Much past research can still be developed for use in the classroom today. We could improve programs and practices significantly if we were simply to know about and develop past research, disseminate development work, and use promising practices.

7. *Additional Research*. While the available research findings have not been used extensively, there is always the need to know more and improve the state of the art. A small but significant number of people are already familiar with all the current research findings and the promising practices in this field. It is hoped that consortia of public schools, universities, and other education agencies will develop in different regions of the country to provide for needed research. Possible kinds of needed research are suggested in Chapter 3.

With the foregoing in mind, let us examine the nature of the behavior of students who are becoming more self-directed and then look at what teachers or schools should be doing to help them along.

Students who are making significant progress toward self-directed learning will:

Want to take increased responsibility for their own learning

Be willing and capable of learning from and with others

Participate in diagnosing, prescribing, and evaluating their own progress

Clarify their values and establish goals consistent with their values

Develop individual and group plans for achieving their goals

Exercise self-discipline

Understand their own learning style and be willing to try other potentially useful learning styles

Become familiar with and know how to use a variety of resources for learning

Be capable of reporting what they have learned in a variety of ways

Know when and how to ask for help or direction from others

Analyze the dynamics of groups and become capable of using group decision-making process.

In addition to the key characteristics cited here, self-directed learners share the need to display characteristics common to all kinds of learners, such as a healthy self-concept (self-respect, self-appreciation), regard for individual rights, and sensitivity to the need to balance off "my" rights against those of other individuals and those of society as a whole. They will also learn to prize human differences, including those related to race, sex, ethnicity, religious affiliation, and social class. Students will use these differences to clarify and develop their own ideas about and their own understandings of self and others.

If students are to learn all the foregoing, in what respects would teacher roles change and how might they behave differently? There are differing degrees of teacher-directedness as there are of self-directedness and so a range of possibilities is described to illustrate the two modes and points between them. The illustrations used are in the areas of: (1) deciding what is to be learned, (2) selecting methods and materials for learning, (3) communicating with others about what is being learned, and (4) evaluating achievement of goals. The labels "school-directed" and "self-directed" as used here do *not* reflect extremes in either case but rather what might be commonly expected in each case. The mid-point category is intended to assist in examining the nature of the changes which might describe the continuum in moving from school-directed to self-directed learning.

Deciding What Is to be Learned

School-Directed: The school and/or teacher select all required subject matter, define all educational goals, and also determine the nature of all elective courses or activities offered.

Mid-point: Students have a voice in selection of subject matter to be learned for at least part of each day or each year. They do this either in required school courses, in selecting certain activities, and/or in proposing what electives should be available.

Self-Directed: Teachers and students cooperatively establish and use criteria for selecting subject matter. These criteria typically take into account goals, current student interests and needs, possible value for college preparation, potential value for career choice and preparation, necessary general citizenship knowledge and skills, and contributions to understanding self and others.

Selecting Method and Materials for Learning

School-Directed: Textbooks and supplementary books are chosen by the school or teacher for use in each field of study. Teachers also select films or other instructional aids and occasionally select speakers and arrange field trips. Students operate in teacher-led activities either in whole-class groups, in small groups, or in individual study.

Mid-point: Teachers give students some options for sources of information and for skills to be learned, or students select their own alternatives with teacher approval.

Self-Directed: Teacher and students, together, examine the various ways of learning and teaching available in school and in the community. Students are helped by teachers and others to find ways of using a variety of methods and materials. Students and teachers establish criteria to determine which methods or combinations of methods are to be used for the particular goals, subject matter, and skills being pursued. Methods criteria can involve trying out new methods to see "how they work for me," improving use of previously used approaches, learning availability of the resources needed (cost, distance), and relevancy of the methods and materials available. Teachers either teach how to use the various methods and materials or assist students in finding ways to learn how to use them.

Communicating With Others About What Is Being Learned

School-Directed: Teachers usually specify one or more of the following in having students indicate what they are learning: written reports, oral reports, completed workbooks or laboratory manuals, and oral or written answers to questions or problems in the textbook.

Mid-point: Students are given a choice of methods of reporting and are encouraged to use different forms of reporting at different times. Students may propose and use other forms of reporting, with consent of the instructor.

Self-Directed: Teachers and students together establish rules for deciding what forms of communicating (reporting) are suitable for the occasion. Rules usually give attention to learning how to use new ways of reporting, how to improve in previously used methods of reporting, what methods are being used by others (to provide for variety), how other members of the class can learn best, and whether certain methods are more appropriate for the content and goals in question. Methods of reporting considered are expanded to include visual and performing arts (arts, crafts, role playing, original drama, tape recording, photographs). Teachers either teach the reporting methods to be used or assist students in finding ways to learn them, as needed.

Evaluating Achievement of Goals

School-Directed: Teachers decide when to assess, what to assess, and how to assess. The most common methods are pre-tests and post-tests, or demonstrations (performing arts, physical education), or products (arts, crafts, homemaking, shop). Primary emphasis in evaluation is on memorization, on recall or on demonstration of skills—within a framework established by the school. Assessment measures are devised or selected by the school. The most recent development is some form of school-determined set of behavioral objectives or competencies.

Mid-point: Teachers provide some latitude for students to determine when they are ready to be tested or allow students to submit plans for alternative ways of measuring achievement of particular competencies. Teachers may also encourage students to submit data to substantiate what each has learned for those times when the students work on personally chosen subjects and goals.

Self-Directed: Teachers and students consider together how to assess knowledge, skills, feelings, interests, and behaviors related to the original goals and topics. Data are gathered for ongoing feedback and at the end of units of study. Assessment measures are selected jointly by students and teachers, utilizing commercially available materials, teacher-devised materials, jointly-developed (teacher-student) measures, and, in some cases, measures developed by students. This process includes teaching students how to use and interpret appropriate diagnostic tests, how to select tests which are valid and reliable, and how to construct assessment measures for cognitive, affective, and psychomotor dimensions of learning.

The ideas, practices, and research described throughout this publication focus primarily on the period from 1930 to the present but other relevant practices could have been cited from at least 100 years ago. To help establish a familiar reference point, the assumptions underlying most of what is written here are probably most closely related to the philosophy of John Dewey. Not the John Dewey perceived by followers of A. S. Neill and his Summerhill School or the John Dewey whom some saw as an American Rousseau, but the person who wrote *Democracy and Education* (Dewey, 1916). In this volume, the "progressive" aspects center on the commitment to the belief that schools must concern themselves with improving the democratic quality of living in this society and faith that human beings are capable of learning to generate these new and improved ways of democratic living. *Democracy and Education* might be viewed as traditionalist in the sense that Dewey believed that the rights of individuals and the rights of society are *inter*-dependent. He shared the optimism of Darwin's belief that the evolution of life is characterized by the survival of the most fit of the species and, by implication, that all humankind has an infinite capacity for improving in all its dimensions. This extends to the capacity for improving the teaching and learning processes. In this view, schools become one of the chief instruments for transformation of this society, and of the individuals in it, to a society operating at successively higher levels of enlightenment.

Self-directed learning, as the authors view it, is rooted in the basic philosophical position that no one can "know" what is "right" for anyone else. Its psychological base is probably best expressed by the authors of ASCD's *Perceiving, Behaving, Becoming* (Combs, 1962). The authors of that ASCD Yearbook stated that educational purposes and perceptions of the nature of the world come from within each individual. All people create the world in which they live. Purposes, perceptions—and potential—are all, literally, unique to each person. In this context, education consists of people helping each other discover what lies within each person and assisting each other in making that potential manifest in living.

Nancy Spencer has summarized this point of view in a position paper entitled "The Development of the Self-Directed Learner as the Aim of Education" (Spencer). The following ideas are drawn from her document:

Learning about the self is an essential part of education: it is learning to grow in the fullest sense. The development of self-directed learners must then include development of a positive view of self as an agent for self-actualization and self-direction.

Adapting and changing through the process of seeking knowledge represents Carl Roger's developmental view of wo(man) involved in non-directive teaching. The individual who is a self-directed learner as a result of this approach to teaching has curiosity, can choose interests and goals, can make responsible choices, . . .

Part of the motivation and capacity to be self-directive results from the gratification of the basic need for self-respect and self-esteem. When the individual has a positive view of self, then (s)he is motivated . . .

Self-direction is only possible when (certain) . . . needs defined by Abraham Maslow (survival, safety, love, ego) have been fulfilled (Goble, 1970).

When an individual has a respect and liking for the self, then it is possible to direct learning experiences that will begin to fulfill the need for self-actualization and self-direction.

. . .The implications of a positive view of self are far reaching. Such a view of self affects school achievement (Combs, 1976; Purkey, 1970); it is instrumental for adults involved in planning their own learning projects (Houle, 1961; Tough, 1971) and for them to be fully functioning beings (Rogers, 1951).

. . . It is because an individual has a positive view of self that (s)he is able to move toward self-actualization, to be less dependent upon others to direct . . . and to plan and implement . . . learning projects.

. . . Self-directed learners do not necessarily need to have an atmosphere created for them in order to explore their own capacities. A positive view of self gives the self-directed learner a portable supportive atmosphere, an aura, that provides . . . a sense of personal power.

Learning is a personal matter. . . . The personal meaning that a self-directed learner discovers in the process of learning . . . becomes that individual's means for achieving his/her chosen ends. Self-directed learners have discovered deep personal meaning in the process of learning. When an individual's perceptual field includes a view of self in the process of learning, and that view has meaning, the learner recognizes why (s)he is . . . and what s(he) is capable of becoming. . . . This knowledge is used to plan future growth through self-directed learning. The consistency of such behavior indicates that the individual is self-actualizing and directing his/her own learning.

Some of the critics of this humanistic psychology describe it as soft, permissive, or fuzzy-minded. These are probably valid criticisms if interpreted to mean that individuals pursue their own purposes and perceptions with little or no regard for other people's goals or views, or if each student's impulses, whims, and wants are indulged without requiring some rationale or criteria for decision making. The irony is that the schools and the teachers who make all decisions for students may be guilty of being "soft" because they do not require students to take increasing responsibility for their own actions and decisions. It *is* being "tough" to require that students participate in making decisions which affect them, particularly if they must be based on some identifiable system of decision making.

While it is popular to describe the world in the language of masculine/feminine power terms ("tough" or "hard," "soft" or "permissive") those emotional terms tend to obscure the real issues. We suggest less time be devoted to such labeling and more to the nature of what we want from our schools. As in the field of consumer education, the label is less important than the quality of the product.

The authors of this publication believe that students *can* learn to be responsible for their own learning, that the degree of their ability to be responsible is a function of the individual's capability (affected by age or stage of development) and that it is also a function of what teachers, parents, and others know about how to help students become self-directed and self-responsible. Needless to say, teachers, principals, and other educators must be moving toward becoming self-directed learners themselves if they hope to succeed in helping students move in this direction.

There have been numerous cases of success by individual teachers and some cases of success by whole schools in promoting self-directed learning. This has occurred with all age groups, beginning with the early elementary school grades. Available research evidence also supports the belief that most students are capable of becoming self-directed.

Among the most promising trends contributing to self-directed learning are the various self-discovery techniques and systems. Young people should be encouraged by parents to examine how they learn before coming to school. Schools should then continue this self-examination of learning processes at each stage of each individual's development. If students become bored with *what* is being learned, they will probably continue to be fascinated with *how* they are learning. Few people lose interest in self as a subject of inquiry. This has implications for teachers in looking at the processes they use for their own learning as well as for their teaching.

If what has been discovered by many individual teachers, by a few schools, and by research were to be gathered together and shared, the state of the art would be improved dramatically. If this were done and if additional needed development and research were to be employed systematically over the next several years in a number of locations, the nature of American education would be changed for the better in significant ways. The democratic character of our whole society would benefit as well.

References

Arthur W. Combs, editor. *Perceiving, Behaving, Becoming: A New Focus for Education.* Washington, D.C.: Association for Supervision and Curriculum Development, 1962.

Arthur W. Combs, A. C. Richards, and F. Richards. *Perceptual Psychology.* New York: Harper and Row, 1976.

John Dewey. *Democracy and Education.* New York: The Macmillan Company, 1951. (Originally published in 1916.)

Frank G. Goble. *The Third Force: The Psychology of Abraham Maslow.* New York: Grossman Publishers, 1970.

C. O. Houle. *The Inquiring Mind.* Madison: University of Wisconsin Press, 1961.

William W. Purkey. *Self-Concept and School Achievement.* Englewood Cliffs, New Jersey: Prentice-Hall, 1970.

Carl R. Rogers. *Client-Centered Therapy.* Boston: Houghton Mifflin, 1951.

Nancy Spencer is the Training Coordinator of the Hampshire Educational Collaborative Title IV-C Project. The position paper is an unpublished document used as a basic reference for that work.

Allen Tough. *The Adult Learning Projects: A Fresh Approach to Theory and Practice in Adult Learning.* Toronto: Ontario Institute for Studies in Education, 1971.

2.
Promising Practices and Relevant Research

Educational movements ebb and flow with varying intensity at different periods in our history. There was the equivalent of a high tide for self-directed learning activities in the heyday of the progressive education movement which reached a crest in the 1930's and early 1940's. It receded drastically as soon as the Russian Sputnik orbited in 1957. Another high tide for student participation in decision making came during the period of college campus "unrest" and then spread to high school "unrest" in the late 1960's.

A counter wave of tidal proportions is now upon us in the form of accountability systems, management systems, competency-based education, grade-level standards, prescriptive learning, teacher-made individual learning plans, and the like. Some are fearful now that the movements toward self-directed learning of the past 50 years will be engulfed and washed away. Such need not happen.

This chapter highlights research findings and promising practices since the 1930's. These represent some well established bases to build on now and to use in the near future when the flood waters of authoritarian movements affecting education have receded.

All items included are judged to be ones which contribute to *some* aspect of self-directed learning. Some deal with only one relatively narrow aspect of all the dimensions of self-directed learning described in the previous chapter (examples include values clarification and moral development). Other items, such as teacher-pupil planning and community-based or citizenship education, potentially involve most of the learning outcomes with which this publication is concerned. All items included are perceived to be relevant today even though some first appeared more than 30 years ago.

11

A. Teacher-Pupil Planning

The core curriculum movement in secondary schools of the late 1930's is one major example of the use of teacher-pupil planning. During the same period, the unit approach and project approach to teaching in elementary schools were being developed in many places in the country. These movements had elements in common, namely, an attempt to correlate or integrate traditional subject matter fields and pupil involvement in some aspect of helping decide what was to be done in school, through planning with each other and with the teacher. The impetus for involvement of students in planning with the teacher was, in part, an outgrowth of Dewey's influence and of the work of the Progressive Education Association. However, it would be oversimplifying to attribute the interest in teacher-pupil planning to any one person or any one cause. The stirrings of liberal, egalitarian forces were evident in many aspects of life in our country during the Depression and, again, shortly after the conclusion of World War II.

Several landmark studies during this time bolstered interest in cooperative teacher-pupil planning. One was the classic Lewin, Lippitt, White study of the effects of adult leadership styles on elementary school age children (White and Lippitt, 1960).

The styles which they compared were described as "democratic," "autocratic," and "laissez-faire." The results tended to favor the democratic which involved adult-child planning, with the autocratic (essentially the traditional adult-directed setting) next most effective, and the laissez-faire approach least effective. Some critics felt that all progressive educators used the laissez-faire style or the "What will we do today, kids?" approach. These critics failed to distinguish between carefully planned involvement of students with teachers, favored by most progressive educators, and the hang-loose, relatively unstructured style espoused by a few of the proponents of progressive education.

Another landmark piece of research involving teacher-pupil planning and reorganization of subject matter was the Eight Year Study which compared the progress of students in experimental programs with those in traditional programs in 30 schools from high school through college from 1933 to 1941 (Aikin, 1942). Each of the 30 schools abandoned the traditional college preparatory curriculum and developed alternative ways of preparing students for success in college. The alternatives varied widely but many of them included unified studies, core curriculum, or life-centered studies. Students were generally allowed latitude either in choice of subjects or participation in planning with teachers *within* classes, or both. The graduates of the 30 schools were compared with graduates of schools which had not departed from the traditional college preparatory track. The students in the experimental schools did as well as or better than their counterparts academically and in leadership roles as well as in athletics and in other extra-curricular aspects of college life. Further analysis indicated that students from the schools which had made the greatest changes from the traditional high school programs were significantly more successful in college, judged by most criteria, than the matched students from the control schools (Aikin, 1942).

The results of the Eight Year Study came out in the midst of war. By the time the nation and its new crop of educators were struggling to return to peacetime activities, few were aware that the research had been done and even fewer pursued its implications for school reform.

The high school core curriculum movement did enjoy a measure of popularity, particularly in and around the schools involved in the Eight Year Study. Research studies were conducted comparing the core curriculum with the more traditional departmentalized subject approach. While the results generally indicated that core curriculum students did as well as or better than students in traditional settings, the research was not as comprehensive or as well defined as could be desired (Vars, 1970; Wright, 1963).

Comprehensiveness was lacking in that most studies of the core curriculum measured only academic achievement and used group achievement tests. Measures of decision-making ability, problem-solving skills, ability to plan, and other factors which were the distinguishing features of the core curriculum were attempted in only a few instances and even then were examined in a relatively superficial manner. Lack of definition arose from the many meanings ascribed to the term "core curriculum." It was sometimes used (incorrectly) to describe one teacher teaching two subjects, usually English and social studies, in a traditional manner with no teacher-pupil planning (block-time classes). It could also be used to describe (appropriately) classes which a teacher conducted for two or three periods, with extensive teacher-pupil planning using a broad-fields approach to subject matter. Most research studies did not distinguish between those radically different approaches. All were lumped together as block-time or core classes.

Several classroom teachers wrote "how to do it" books based on their successful experiences in carrying out teacher-pupil planning. Among them were *Teacher-Pupil Planning for Better Classroom Learning* (Parrish and Waskin, 1958) and *Democratic Processes in the Secondary Classroom* (Zapf, 1959). Both books contain descriptions of practices which were not only successful in their time but are also promising practices for the present. Two more recent publications in this field should also be noted: *Students as Partners in Team Learning* (Poirier, 1970) and *Teaching, Loving, and Self-Directed Learning* (Thatcher, 1973). Teacher-pupil planning has generally been used more often in elementary schools than in secondary schools. For those who may be interested in catching an educational cycle at its peak, the next appearance of general popular interest in teacher-pupil planning is likely to occur in 3-5 years as a reaction to current directive approaches.

B. Community-Based Educational Programs and Citizenship Education

In the 1930's, a number of educators and community people initiated the community school movement based on the premise that the *total* community educates its young, that schools represent one important part of this educative process, and consequently schools and the other educative agencies of the community should coordinate efforts for this common purpose. The original community school movement and other more recent examples of community-based education programs include the belief that the curriculum should focus more on present issues and real problems in the community and engage students in working with community people on improving the quality of life in the community. That philosophy can be summed up by saying that *the best preparation for the future is to successfully deal with today's issues and problems today*. One of the first conceptualizations of how a community school might operate was described by Archibald Shaw (1956) in his detailed description of the "Random Falls" plan.

While Random Falls was a mythical place, many of the programs and practices described there were based on actual activities going on at that time in a number of locations in our country. One novel feature was that each student in this proposed four-year high school was required to spend one quarter of each year in some kind of community service role, either in the immediate home area or in the community of an exchange program school. High school seniors, for example, would spend one quarter of their senior year in community service in an underdeveloped country. (This concept was proposed before the advent of the Peace Corps.)

Community-based ·educational programs have become much more popular in recent years and hundreds of illustrations of successful practices and programs are now being reported (National Commission on Resources for Youth, 1974; Tyler, 1978; National Association of Secondary School Principals, 1974).

The major significance of community-based educational programs for those interested in promoting self-directed learning is that students take on real rather than simulated responsibilities in some community activity. What they do, under school direction, makes a difference now in their own lives and/or in the lives of others in their community. Examples of community-based activities include sixth-grade students reading to the elderly in a retirement home in Mill Valley, California; high school students being trained at a health clinic to give talks to their agemates and younger people about drug use, nutrition, and mental health in Minneapolis, Minnesota; teenagers in Cornwall-on-Hudson, New York, operating a natural science museum for the community; Navajo youth in Utah interviewing older people in their tribe to preserve their tribal history on films and in books; students in the New Voter Project in Marin County, California, helping register new voters, developing materials for proposed new ordinances, and working on community environmental education projects; students in a racially mixed eighth grade room in River Rouge, Michigan, selecting for study the topic, "How Can We Improve Race Relations in This Class?".

Citizenship education has co-existed with community-based education and the two sets of activities overlap in nature. One of the first comprehensive reports on citizenship education which described courses of study, effective procedures in classroom teaching and learning, out-of-school activities, school-community relationships, and democratic school administration appeared in 1940 in the Educational Policies Commission's *Learning the Ways of Democracy: A Case Book of Civic Education* (National Education Association, 1940).

In its 1951 Yearbook, the National Council for the Social Studies described a number of projects, research studies, in-service education workshops, and accompanying instructional materials then in existence for the purpose of learning how to teach students to be more effective members of a democratic society. Much of value was developed in these projects. Chief among them were the Syracuse Citizenship Education Conference; the three-year Cambridge Civic Education Project sponsored by the Educational Research Corporation in 1948; the five-year Detroit Citizenship Education Study begun in 1944 with an initial grant of $85,000; the Kansas Study of Education for Citizenship funded by a grant of $240,000; and the Citizenship Education Project at Teachers College, Columbia University, established in 1949 with an initial grant of $50,000 and with supplemental grants of $400,000 and $958,000 to carry through 1953 (National Council for the Social Studies, 1951, pp. 110-23). The activities and projects reported produced results which were helpful then and which would still be of interest to many people today. The amounts of funding are cited to illustrate the major commitments of money for those times.

Continuing national interest in citizenship education extended through the late 1950's and these activities were reported in another Yearbook of the National Council for the Social Studies, *Citizenship and a Free Society: Education for the Future.* The editor of that publication, Franklin Patterson, then Director of the Tufts Civic Education Center, argued that, "Our task is to find a way to move education from a relatively inert role in the social order to one of leadership in social change" though *not* ". . . by increasing our schools' output of qualified scientists and technologists" (National Council for the Social Studies, 1960, pp. 14, 15).

One of the most salient points made in relation to self-directed learning appears in Chapter XI of the NCSS 1951 Yearbook in which Erling Hunt summarizes results of elementary and secondary school programs for citizenship education. He emphasizes five points regarding citizenship education, "First: information is indispensable. Second: information is not enough; understanding, skills, attitudes, and behavior . . . must also have explicit . . . attention. Third: citizenship education is an all-school and all-community responsibility. . . . Fourth: democratic citizenship should be practiced, not merely talked about . . . ; young people should be encouraged to exercise initiative and allowed to exercise responsibility. Fifth: . . . all school workers . . . have guidance responsibilities" (pp. 122-23).

In analyzing community-based and citizenship education, the major difference between them appears to be the emphasis of the role of schools and the role of the community in education. The need to have community and schools working together actively in education and to have students engaged in community projects is common to both. The philosophic difference might be the notion that the *community educates* and schooling is one part of community education on the one hand, and the belief that *schools educate* by making active use of the community on the other.

Both sets of concepts are relevant to self-directed learning in that they call for students to:

1. Take increased responsibility for their own learning as they select projects to work on in the community

2. Develop individual and group plans for achieving goals

3. Clarify values and establish goals consistent with their values

4. Exercise self-discipline needed to carry out school and community projects

5. Become familiar with the wide variety of school resources and community resource materials needed to carry out "live," ongoing projects

6. Learn how to report to others in various ways about what their findings are

7. Discover when and how to ask for help as it is needed

8. Be capable of participating with other students and with adults in group decision-making processes.

Students of all races and ethnic groups, of both sexes, of all social class backgrounds, from every region of the United States, and from city, suburban, and rural areas are providing evidence every day that young people can take on what we usually refer to as "adult" responsibility and do so creditably. This should not be surprising when we consider that in many parts of the world today there is no word or phrase for adolescence. People begin to participate as full-fledged members of the adult society when they are as young as 10, 11, or 12 years of age—as they did in our own country until the turn of this century. It is easy to mistake lack of *opportunity* for responsibility for lack of *capability* for responsibility, particularly in technologically advanced and relatively affluent countries like our own.

C. Values Clarification and Moral Education

The question of what is "right" and/or "right for me" must be addressed in making decisions, regardless of the age of the person doing so. The work of Louis Raths, Sidney Simon, and others in values clarification and of Lawrence Kohlberg and his associates in moral education are the most widely known attempts to help provide answers to this question through school-based efforts.

Both systems have been used in a number of locations, the results have been viewed with favor in most of these situations, and there is research evidence to support claims of effectiveness. Research shows that students can learn to understand and to state what they believe in (life values) and to behave in ways that are consistent with those beliefs. Although the two approaches have much in common, some basic differences in assumptions underlie each and those differences are important to those of us who are interested in self-directed learning.

Values clarification experiences are designed to help students *discover* what their values are and the role of teachers is to facilitate this process but not to shape which values are chosen. The teacher is active as a co-equal participant in stating views and directs the processes used, but actively discourages having anyone be in a dominant role in determining what the "right" values are or which ones are of most worth. The emphasis is on individual self-discovery and self-assertiveness with equal regard for the rights of others to hold their own values and to act on them (Simon *et al.*, 1972).

Kohlberg, on the other hand, describes stages of moral development arranged in a hierarchical fashion from "level one" to "level six." Each successive level is perceived as being superior to the preceding one. In his view, while moral growth tends to be associated with other growth and development of young people, almost all people become fixed at one level in a particular stage of their moral development and this fixing takes place at a different age for each person. Fewer and fewer people will ever arrive at each of the successive higher levels (particularly the two highest levels) and, finally, people at each stage of moral development find it difficult, perhaps impossible, even to understand the moral viewpoints of persons who are two levels or more beyond their own level of development. The role of the teacher in the Kohlberg model is to encourage students to make progress from one level to another, or to help them direct themselves toward higher levels of moral development (Kohlberg, 1970).

In deciding which approach is more appropriate, if just one is to be used, the user should be aware of the potential shortcomings of each. Values clarification is criticized as fostering the notion that all values are of equal worth or that "anything goes." Many parents object to exposing their children to other sets of beliefs—particularly those which may challenge moral/religious values held by the parents.

Kohlberg's moral education is sometimes criticized as being too limiting, both in purporting to describe *all* of the major moral viewpoints worthy of consideration and also in implying that there should be indoctrination of students according to one person's opinion of which sets of beliefs ("levels" of moral education) are inherently superior to others.

Jan Tucker identifies three other values-education approaches in use today, namely, "evocation and union," "value analysis," and "action learning." However, values clarification and moral development are perhaps the most widely discussed approaches and, with various modifications, probably the most widely used. While a fair amount of research has been conducted in this field, it has been inadequate in scope and methodology for the teacher or other educator who is looking for the particular elements which are most likely to contribute to specified learning outcomes (Tucker, 1977). More will be said about this in Chapter 3.

Another major program for helping students decide what is "right" for them to do is Ralph Ojemann's work done on "causal" teaching in the 1940's when he was Chief of the Child Welfare Research Station at Iowa State University. Ojemann was trying to find ways to prevent mental illness by teaching students to understand the "why" of human behavior, both their own and that of others around them. He developed materials for use in teaching traditional subjects at both the elementary and secondary school levels. Research on its use in public school classrooms indicated that significant improvement resulted in pupil understanding of the causes of human behavior and that subject matter was learned as well as or better than when traditional methods and materials were used (Ojemann, 1970). As with much of the research and successful application reported here, few people even know of his work and fewer still have made use of it despite the fact that it takes little time to learn to do and costs very little to carry out.

The efforts related to values clarification, moral education, and causal teaching all are designed to illustrate the basic principle that all behavior is *caused*, that the causes are discernible, and that awareness of the bases for behavior will help individuals and groups to establish more valid goals and make wiser decisions. It would seem that values clarification or its equivalent *must* precede goal setting and all other activities related to self-directed learning. Logically this makes sense: how can wise choices be made if the decision-maker does not have a clear notion of personal priorities for living? Psychologically, few people follow a linear process of establishing values→ setting goals consistent with those values→selecting activities to achieve the goals, and so on. Discovery of personal values, moral principles, and other causes of human behavior *are* important to all other aspects of self-directed learning. However, the discovery processes are unfolding and dynamic ones, even with the use of the best of currently available skills and knowledge. Part of this is due to what we are capable of understanding at various ages, part to the complexity of each person's nature, and part to changes which regularly occur in individuals as a consequence of social interaction. The most important aspects of the processes involved have to do with *self*-discovery and *self*-awareness.

D. Establishment of Achievable Goals, Self-Discipline, and Self-Assessment

Teacher-pupil planning often includes establishing class goals (or goals for a teaching unit). It has been widely used in the core curriculum, in the unit approach to teaching, and in class projects, as described in an earlier portion of this chapter.

Work by David McClelland at Harvard on achievement motivation and follow-up efforts by Alfred Alschuler in the 1960's on teaching students to be achievement-motivated give special attention to learning how to define *achievable* goals and proceed to carry them out. Achievement motivation teaching was first employed by McClelland with business people in India to help them become successful in business. Using the same principles, achievement-motivation techniques were developed and used effectively in public secondary schools (Alschuler *et al.*, 1970). The same principles could be applied in elementary schools as well.

Alschuler and others have gone on to develop ways of promoting self-discipline in the achievement of goals through what they call social literacy training. In this training, teachers and students together examine the behavior of students and the system of schooling to determine causes of discipline problems and to formulate methods for improving discipline (Alschuler *et al.*, 1977).

A number of publications have provided excellent guidelines for promoting self-discipline. Among these is the ASCD booklet by George Sheviakov and Fritz Redl (1944) published more than 30 years ago and widely used. It continued to sell so well that it was revised for the Association by Sybil K. Richardson in 1956 and is still a best-seller.

The third ingredient in carrying out goals (after learning how to define achievable goals and maintain self-discipline) is knowing how to self-assess progress made.

Self-assessment was given great impetus by the work of Ralph Tyler in formulating his concept of behavioral objectives, first utilized extensively in his evaluation procedures for the Eight Year Study (Aikin, 1942).

In teacher-pupil planning, students and teachers ask, "What would we look like if we were to achieve this goal?"; "What would we be able to do, say, write, etc., that we cannot do now?". In developing skills of group decision making the question might be, "What does a person look like when he/she is an *effective* member of a group involved in decision making?". To establish a continuum, two other questions might be asked: "What does a person look like when she/he is completely ineffective as a member of such a group?" and "What does someone do who is somewhere in between being completely ineffective and highly effective in a decision making group?". Use of behavioral objectives to clarify goals, to help identify useful learning experiences, and to check on work in progress (formative evaluation) can be useful. Recent uses of behavioral objectives by federal, state, and local education agencies as major means for evaluating achievement of goals (summative evaluation) are *not* advocated for use in programs for self-directed learning.

Another likely source of self-assessment techniques resides in conversion of techniques for assessment of students *by teachers* to assessment of students *by themselves*. Most of these teacher-diagnostic techniques can be used in their present form for older youth to learn how to use, or can be adapted and simplified for younger students.

Self-assessment activities have been devised for use with almost every conceivable goal. Relatively little has been done to date, however, in devising assessment of each major educational goal in terms of all three dimensions of humanness (cognitive, affective, and psychomotoric). The emphasis has been on the cognitive and to a lesser extent on the motoric aspects but relatively little on the affective. This is true despite the fact that how we feel about what we do and know is always important and is often the dominating aspect of our being. Teaching, including that for self-directed learning, could improve dramatically if more teachers would examine their thinking, feeling, and acting simultaneously in every dimension of education beginning with goal setting and extending through evaluation of achievement.

E. Increasing Students' Options for Learning Activities

The nature of the learning activities provided by schools helps establish the limits of what can be learned. We obviously cannot foster creativity in schools unless students have an opportunity to display creative thinking. Similarly, we cannot expect to witness scientific problem solving, democratic decision making, scholarly essay writing, or acceptance of people of other races and ethnic groups unless students both observe and participate actively in productive experiences directly relating to these goals.

At least three areas of promise for increasing the individual student potential for learning have emerged from research studies of the past 20 years.

These are the studies of creativity, of intellectual processes (Guilford) and "split-brain" research findings.

Complementary research in the 1950's by Jacob Getzels and Philip Jackson at the University of Chicago and by J. P. Guilford at the University of Southern California led to the finding that most school activities make use of only a small portion of the intellectual processes students are capable of displaying. For example, Guilford identified some 120 intellectual processes or factors which humans can utilize. But, traditional achievement tests and intelligence tests call for use of only some five to fifteen of these factors. Traditional classroom activities also use few of these factors, most of which fall under the rubric of "convergent" thinking, that is, relying on memorization, simple recall, deductive reasoning, and simple application of known facts. Very little in school operation or in standardized tests calls for "divergent" thinking, that is, "generation of information . . . where the emphasis is upon variety and quantity of output from the same source" (Guilford, 1967).

Getzels and Jackson, who worked with children at the University of Chicago Elementary School, found that students who had the highest scores on intelligence tests were often not the same students who had the highest scores on tests of creativity. When students in the upper fifth of each set of scores were compared, only about one third of the students were found on both lists. In comparing students who were on one list but not on the other, the "high-I.Q." students more often held values they viewed as being consistent with those of their parents and of other adults, placed less value on a good sense of humor, were more likely to be chosen by teachers as desirable students, and were more likely to receive higher grades (despite the fact that the achievement scores of "high-I.Q." and "high-creative" students were comparable). Significant differences in child-rearing practices also emerged in comparing the "high-I.Q." and "high-creative" students (Getzels and Jackson, 1962).

The implications of these research studies for self-directed learning are that the nature of teaching methods, materials, and content needs to be expanded radically in order to capitalize on just the academic potential of students—*even of Anglo, middle-class students whom the schools have traditionally afforded the greatest opportunity for success.* The scholastic, (cognitive) part of schooling is under-utilized. In advocating a return to the basics, those who are doing so probably are neglecting as much as 90 percent of the cognitive, scholastic, "tough" part of what schooling could be. This omission is being corrected by Mary Nacol Meeker (1969) and others in proposing classroom activities for all of Guilford's 120 intellectual processes.

Other dimensions of human potential appear in split-brain research findings. *Education and the Brain,* a Yearbook of the National Society for the Study of Education (Chall and Mersky, 1978), summarizes work on the nature of the brain in all the education-related aspects from a cross-disciplinary view. Bob Samples (1976) has extracted for classroom use some of the research findings from studies on the "other half" of the brain. Scattered reports indicate that practices based on split-brain research are effective, both with underachieving and slow learning children as well as with more academically able youngsters. Some enthusiastic proponents claim more about the potential of this movement than available data would warrant at this point. However, it is an area of investigation which is certainly worthy of further study.

All educators have much to learn from what is now known about fostering creativity, about the nature of intellectual process, and about the findings concerning the "other half" of the brain. These kinds of research findings have special significance for those who want to engage students actively in their own learning. The potential for what might result if only the teacher had this information to use with students is great. However, if individual students were able to learn how to discover and use it to help each other learn, the results could be even more exciting. With assistance from teachers, results might be beyond our ability to conceive of at this time.

F. Learning About Learning Styles*

"Learning style" is a broad, general term defined in many ways. Learning style, as used in this section, is the personally preferred way of dealing with information and experience for learning that crosses content areas. *Your* style is *you* in action in all aspects of life. All writers, regardless of the terminology used or the parameters emphasized, are in agreement that one's style affects one's view of the world and one's resultant learning and behavior.

An essential part of the self-knowledge necessary for self-directed learning is the knowledge of one's own learning style. Herb Thelen (1954), the father of investigations in learning styles, suggests that "the most significant quality of a good teacher is that he is able to meet his own needs through playing the roles required to make activities educative for students. . . . Learning by students is complicated by the facts that different kinds of learning require different roles, and that learning experience is complex, involving thoughts, feelings, actions, emotions, and desires" (p. 41). Thelen suggests that teachers know not only their own learning styles, but also those of the students. Thelen also suggests continuous diagnosis during teaching to achieve a reality-centered education that relates to three basic aspects of teaching: "conscious problem solving, group process, and individual meaning" (p. 50). This raises the question of how one can identify learning styles.

*Section F was prepared by Anthony Gregorc, University of Connecticut, Storrs, with the assistance of graduate student Judy Krupp. The portion on cognitive mapping was prepared by James Orr and James Berry.

Numerous researchers have studied learning styles. Witkin (1954), Kagan and Wright (1963), and Hunt (1972) all discuss the field-independent or field-dependent person. The field-dependent person has a global environmental view. Such a person is relational and subjective and often enjoys social studies and the humanities. The field-independent individual is an analytic, objective person who controls his/her environment. Such an individual may prefer the sciences.

Weisgerber (1971) discusses other dimensions of learning style. These include degree of attention or scanning ability, breadth of categorizing, conceptualizing styles, cognitive simplicity or complexity, leveling to see commonalities or sharpening to see differences, reflectiveness or impulsivity, constricted or flexible control, and tolerance for incongruous or unrealistic experience. Kagan (1971) adds a tenth style, risk-taking versus cautiousness.

To complicate the picture further, Smith, Bodoin, and Bentley (1975) suggest that learning style involves sensory factors such as visual, tactile, and auditory receptivity; human interaction factors such as group size, people-people, people-things, and people-action relationships; and other factors such as timing, temperature, time of day, and hunger.

Rosenberg (1968) has studied learning style as the locus of information and the level of symbolization employed. The locus of information can be intrapersonal or extrapersonal according to Rosenberg and the level of symbolism can be concrete or abstract. Four styles result: rigid-inhibited, undisciplined, acceptance-anxious, and the creative person. Rosenberg hypothesizes that the effectiveness of a style depends upon the amount of material that can be processed and that the amount increases in direct proportion to one's abstract ability over the value for concrete ability.

Given this complexity and diversity of categorization how is a teacher to diagnose learning styles? Observation of behavior, observation of errors, interviews, and inventories can be used by a teacher to diagnose learning styles. Cross (1976) gives excellent suggestions about observations and interviews. Numerous authors present inventories which are accessible, easy to administer, and represent a composite of the numerous learning style characteristics enumerated here.

Dunn and Dunn (1972) provide a learning style questionnaire that is geared to the child. The child is asked about environmental stimuli such as sound, light, temperature, and design; emotional stimuli such as motivation, persistence, responsibility, and structure; sociological stimuli such as degree of aloneness; and physical stimuli such as perceptual preferences, food intake, time, and mobility. After the child has completed the questionnaire, the child and teacher have more knowledge of the many parameters in that child's learning process. A child who prefers to work with others in a brightly lighted area and who needs to move about can be given different means of achieving a learning task from the one who likes to work alone in a brightly lighted area and who is sedentary and perservering. Such knowledge of self is the foundation for self-directed learning.

Anthony Gregorc (1977) offers a learning style inventory geared to adults. His test places four scores for the adult on a graph:

The adult is placed according to the degree of concreteness or abstractness and degree of randomness or sequentialness in learning source preference. The resultant behavioral preference is then discussed. An "abstract sequential" person (AS), for example, decodes abstract symbols well, whereas the "concrete sequential" person (CS) prefers a direct sense-related, hands-on experience. Understanding of these traits in oneself as the teacher, and in the child, results in learning that is based on more than ability or achievement testing. When the abstract sequential person is enjoying the lecture the teacher has so carefully prepared, the abstract random person may be looking out the window, reading the bulletin board, or wishing to discuss the topic rather than listen to a lecture. Ability aside, achievement is related to use of one's learning style or ability to adjust that style.

Simon and Byram (1977) have enclosed within their book a "Communicating Styles Survey" by Paul Mok. The test gives information about one's learning style under favorable and under stress conditions. The four styles are called "feeler," "thinker," "sensor," and "intuitor." The test, geared to the older student or adult learner, is particularly applicable to the teacher's learning style. Simon and Byram describe a precise way for a teacher to establish a student learning style profile. Little time is needed to do so and the results are rewarding.

An instrument directly applicable to teaching style is available in the work of Smith *et al.* (1975). The instrument places a teacher on a continuum for *influence*, from direct and dominating to indirect and facilitating; for *management*, from laissez-faire to business-like structure (reminiscent of Lewin, Lippitt, and White's work); for *relatedness*, from personal and close to impersonal and distant; for *tone*, from intense and dramatic to subdued and quiet; and for *operations*, from concrete to abstract.

The authors also provide a more general learning style checklist that is applicable to children as well as adults. It includes sections dealing with parameters of learning style such as intellectually-directed, emotionally-directed, methodical-structured, open-structured, sensory, multiple-sensory, independent, social, slow-paced and rapidly-paced styles. A slow-paced child with a rapidly-paced teacher can result in conflict, unless both persons are consciously aware of their learning style differences. Ten minutes may be sufficient for one child to complete a learning task, but another equally able child who is more random may require twenty minutes.

Regardless of which of these test devices a teacher may choose or whether the teacher chooses to observe behavior, study student errors, interview, or use all four techniques, it is imperative that teachers be aware of the learning style of students and their own teaching and learning style; that students be aware of their own learning style and those of the teachers; and that the principal be aware of his/her own learning style and those of the teachers. Such awareness results in greater self-direction and greater sensitivity. It permits each individual to recognize that each learning style has extremes, but each is adaptive for different needs. It permits a teacher to discuss a topic in terms that are more readily understandable to a student. It reinforces the need expressed so well by Joyce and Weil (1972) to provide multiple ways for the teacher to reach the learner. A teacher may provide concrete examples, a movie, a riddle, or a book all on the same topic and permit the learner to choose the learning approach that is most comfortable.

Learning styles result from a composite of environmental and inherited factors. According to Smith et al. (1975), they are a result of experience; psychologic, neurologic, and physiologic factors; habit; training; models; and value preferences. Anthony Gregorc (1977) suggests three types of learning style proclivities: First, there is natural ability that is inherent in the individual; second, there are synthetic strengths which are learned, approximate the natural, and become an integral part of the individual; and third, artificial proclivities exist which approximate the natural and are added on. Cross (1976) suggests that there is some evidence that cognitive styles remain throughout life and that the emphasis should be on helping students diversify their strategies.

The awareness of the learning style of all persons involved in a learning situation can result in emphasis on the strengths of an individual or in style-flexing, sometimes called diversification of strategies. Both are essential. Style-flexing refers to the ability of an individual to use a learning style that is appropriate to a situation but different from the most comfortable one. Teachers can style-flex in two ways. They can change their behavior to communicate using all styles, as suggested earlier. Second, they can help children be more flexible in their behaviors by presenting the topic in one mode, but giving warm supportive help to those who are "stretching" their learning style. The use of the first technique helps the child utilize an area of strength, but requires the teacher to stretch into unaccustomed teaching styles. Use of an area of strength is important to sense of self and makes the learning of new cognitive or affective material easier for the student. The teacher is required to demonstrate "responsive flexibility," that is, the ability to change as the situation changes (Smith et al.). The second technique helps a child stretch and develop abilities that may be needed when that child must think about new situations. For example, if a concrete-sequential child has a teacher who is abstract-random, or a "thinking" child meets a "feeling" teacher, then the child's ability to adjust will be directly related to how well that child can style-flex. A child may call on another child who has a different learning style proclivity to help stretch. A fine explanation of style-flexing, complete with concrete examples geared to teachers, can be found in the book by Simon and Byram (1977).

Learning style materials are vital to the self-directed learner for another reason. They provide a vocabulary and a way of thinking that emphasizes flexibility and understanding of individual differences, thus improving the quality of human interaction. The child with a proclivity for risk-taking (concrete-random) can more easily understand a disagreement if aware that another student is abstract-random and wants a great deal of information from many sources before making a decision. Respect for differences defuses disagreements that are often based upon defense of one's self. A teacher using a concrete-sequential learning technique, such as a hands-on science experiment without previous reading by the student, might spend five minutes discussing with the abstract-sequential student why this may be a difficult assignment, thus leading to more self-understanding and respect for the individual and ultimately to self-directed learning. Even discipline problems can be handled easily with knowledge of learning styles. A child who is daydreaming might simply need a comment such as "John, this approach is concrete-sequential and your abstract-random ability is causing difficulty. How about trying to stretch?"

Hilda Taba, as early as 1932, criticized our schools because the learner and the psychological process of learning are both subordinated to the learning materials or to external stimulation. Knowledge of learning styles and application of that knowledge places the emphasis on the learner and the psychological process of learning.

For learning to result in an "emitted response," as Carl Rogers (1969) would call one that originates in the learner, knowledge of learning style is imperative. Without such knowldge one may be limited to an "elicited response." An elicited response, according to Rogers, is one brought about by an external stimulus. The responsibility for learning rests with the student, but the teacher must encourage the student to achieve as much self-knowledge as possible so that the student can have confidence in self-directed abilities.

Another way of looking at learning styles has been formulated by Joseph Hill (1976), and is sometimes referred to as "cognitive mapping." The following information is drawn from material submitted for this publication by James Orr and James Berry of Oakland Community College, Bloomfield Hills, Michigan:

"Educational cognitive mapping is a process which identifies elements of a person's educational cognitive style. . . . The cognitive map is a pictorial representation of an educational cognitive style." Individual cognitive style derives from each person's (1) symbolic orientations, (2) cultural determinants, and (3) modalities of inference.

The first set of elements mapped is related to symbolic orientations. For example, does the individual gain meaning by reading or listening? Does the individual gain meaning from concrete sensory experiences? Also identified is the person's capacity for empathy, the ability to enjoy the beauty of an object or an idea, and the nature of commitment to a particular set of values, principles, obligations, and/or duties.

The second group of elements explored is termed cultural determinants. The relative influence of family, associates (peers), and one's own individuality are identified.

The third group of elements is identified as the modalities of inference. This group defines the ways the individual reaches decisions or comes to conclusions: does the person look for one-to-one contrasts and, therefore, seek differences or is an attempt made to synthesize data to reach a conclusion? All of these elements are represented in a cognitive style map which is depicted here:

$$
\begin{matrix} \text{Educational} \\ \text{Cognitive Style} \end{matrix} = \left\{ \begin{matrix} \text{Symbolic} \\ \text{Orientation} \end{matrix} \right\} X \left\{ \begin{matrix} \text{Cultural} \\ \text{Determinants} \end{matrix} \right\} X \left\{ \begin{matrix} \text{Modalities} \\ \text{of Inference} \end{matrix} \right\}
$$

The format of the map indicates that it is necessary for the teacher to include each set of information in mapping a young person's educational cognitive style.

The educational cognitive style of an individual is not fixed but is considered to be augmentable and modifiable by educational experiences. Furthermore, educational cognitive style is a relative concept that is related to the level of educational development of the individual, the cultural background of the individual, and the educational task confronting that person. A study by Ogden and Brewster (1977) found that differences in academic performance of high school students in science classes were related to their educational cognitive style and grade level.

For any student, knowledge of one's educational cognitive style allows one to understand the methods and materials used in the learning process.

Individual students can reach a stage of self-matching for their own learning needs. For a teacher, information from educational cognitive style mapping identifies ways of knowing beyond those measured and found in traditional intelligence and aptitude tests.

Teachers who use the educational sciences approach in the classroom need to be aware of their own educational cognitive style. When both the teacher and student are aware of each other's cognitive style, communication and learning are enhanced. Further, teachers increase their understanding of the student as a learner and as a person. Educational cognitive style helps the teacher to become more aware of the alternative ways of facilitating self-directed learning for students (Hill, 1976).

G. Individualization Through Grouping Practices and Independent Study

Two of the most commonly used practices for individualizing instruction in recent years have been homogeneous (ability) grouping and various forms of independent study.

Sometimes what we learn from research and from practice is what *not* to do. This is particularly true in looking at the results of ability grouping. It is quite clear that homogeneous grouping does not yield the results for which it is usually established, namely, reduction in the range of individual differences, better provision for individual learning, and, above all, increased learning for both high-ability and low-ability students. Among the conclusions in one 1968 review of research on ability grouping was that after some 40 years of extensive research, "the results were inconclusive and indefinite," and further that "Available evidence indicates that factors other than ability grouping *per se* may account for the many differences in achievement test results" (NEA Research Bulletin, 1968).

An elaborate and comprehensive study of ability grouping was conducted by Miriam Goldberg, Harry Passow, and Joseph Justman in 86 classrooms in New York City and results were reported in 1966. Goldberg concluded "No matter how precise the selection of students becomes . . . grouping arrangements, by themselves, serve little educational purpose. Real differences in academic growth result from what is taught and learned in the classroom" (p. 169).

What has all this to do with self-directed learning? The unfounded belief that ability grouping aids in learning leads to its use in establishing class sections and is also the chief basis for establishing homogeneous small groups within the class. This myth is potentially a deterrent to developing programs for self-directed learning in that there is also a prevalent tacit assumption that high academic ability and ability to be self-responsible are almost synonymous. There are no empirical data to support this belief. It is a self-fulfilling prophecy to anticipate that students with lower I.Q. scores and/or lower achievement test scores are less able to be self-responsible and self-directed in learning. That unwarranted anticipation may set unreasonably high expectations for one group and unreasonably low ones for others. It also fails to take into account the value of having students of varying abilities learn from each other.

The research findings from cross-age tutoring experiences, cited later in this chapter, support the notion that both (or all) parties involved benefit from such tutoring processes. The broad goals which are characteristic of programs for self-directed learning (group process skills, planning skills; comparing, contrasting, and selecting learning styles, to name a few) require great diversity in individual differences in a classroom. The current mania for narrowly and precisely defined objectives in homogeneously-grouped classes will, more likely, produce narrow, precisely defined, and homogeneous groups of citizens than better-educated ones.

Other negative aspects of ability grouping are obvious to people who are in daily contact with schools. How often do we hear, "These are my *good* kids" or "This is my *poor* group"? The labeling which results is demeaning to the students who are classed as "the dummies" as well as to those who are regarded as the elite. To compound the problem, when ability groups are formed in schools which draw from heterogeneous populations, the class sections formed tend to become racial and/or social class groupings. The issue of the relation of social-cultural forces to self-directed learning is treated at greater length in Chapter 4.

Research and practice strongly suggest that heterogeneous groups are more likely to foster the kinds of learnings with which this publication is concerned, whether the heterogeneous groups are small groups within a class or are the basis for establishing the whole class section. Teachers who wish to cope successfully with the wide range of normal differences in learning will benefit from learning how to teach students to help each other and also in learning to teach students how to individualize their own instruction.

Independent study is another popular approach to individualization of instruction which can assist in self-directed learning if it is viewed as one mode in an array of learning styles used by each student. James Wells* contributes the following in support of independent study:

• The literature has treated independent study extensively beginning in the late 1950's and continuing to the present. . . . Among the chief values claimed for independent study, Felder (1964) found that the following were supported: it develops responsibility and independence in learning, provides

---

*James D. Wells, Associate Professor, Florida International University, Miami, prepared an overview of independent study practices from which this material is excerpted.

more adequately for individual differences, and enables students to explore subjects in greater depth.

• Baskin (1960) summarized the results of academic examinations of students in independent study and pointed out that they learned at least as much as students who had regular classwork.

• Beggs and Buffie (1957) edited a book dealing with the theory underlying independent study, descriptions of programs, and suggestions for introducing and implementing independent study.

• Probably the most comprehensive survey and treatment to date has been the work of Alexander, Hines, and associates (1967).

• Plunkett (1975), a high school director of independent study, describes a career exploration program where students serve as volunteer workers as yet another option for students to become self-directed learners.

• One of the continuing problems related to independent study is a confusion or lack of acceptance of a generally agreed upon definition.

• Wells (1966) has classified the many and varied independent study practices into ten types based upon administrative arrangements in relationship to instructional organization. The ten types are:

1. Some released time given from a regular class so that some students may work independently on individually planned studies in addition to class assignments

2. Some released time given from a regular class so that some students may work independently on individually planned studies in lieu of class assignments

3. Seminar groups which are smaller than ordinary classes in which students work independently, at least part of the time, on common or individual topics, units, or problems

4. Individually planned programs of curricular study with regularly scheduled time to study independently, in or out of school, with a minimum of teacher direction and supervision

5. Independent study as a part of a program of instruction organized around large- and small-group instruction

6. Individual, extracurricular enrichment study with students working independently before or after school or on weekends (school facilities open mornings, nights, or weekends)

7. Vocational or work experience programs of instruction in which students work independently, in or out of school, so that they will develop salable skills

8. A curricular program which emphasizes the development of student responsibility in regard to the individual's use of regularly offered independent study time

9. A regularly scheduled class in the school's instructional program which normally requires that students work independently (for example, school publications, advanced courses in art, industrial arts, music) as individual members of a regular class.

10. A regularly scheduled class in the school's instructional program which provides all students with some independent study time in order to accomplish a long-term class assignment required of all members of the class but which may be individually planned in terms of the specific topic or problem studied.

• Teachers in core curriculum or block-time interdisciplinary programs have historically sought additional methods for increasing students' self-directed learning. A variety of approaches are used for initiating and developing independent study in a core setting (Wells, 1969).

• In summary, if one of the major purposes of independent study is the provision of opportunities to learn to make intelligent choices and to learn to learn on one's own, then it would appear that this method of providing for self-directed learning needs to be given increased attention, encouragement, and support.

There are many other approaches to individualization of instruction which have meaning for self-directed learning but which space limitations do not allow for consideration of at this time. Ability grouping has been cited because of its widespread use and great popularity. *When combined with competency-based programs, the result is a major deterrent to self-directed learning.* The reason is that most so-called "competency-based" programs rely on observation of pieces of human behavior viewed separately, atomistically. Ability grouping categorizes students into types of human beings based on selected predetermined characteristics (grades, I.Q. scores). The combination of the two compounds stereotyping and limits what the teacher is able to develop in students. It also limits what students can expect to observe in their own educational development. Not only can the result be dehumanizing and demeaning to the participants, it severely restricts the possibility that either the teacher or the student can come to know or develop individual and group potential for learning, in all their richness and complexity.

Independent study is gaining in popularity as a means of individualizing instruction, particularly in secondary schools and colleges. If used in combination with small peer-group planning, and teacher-pupil planning, it can provide an additional option for student self-directed learning. However, independent study should be viewed as only one of a set of modes of learning that individual students may employ at any age level.

H. Using Social Class, Race, Ethnicity, and Sex

Chapter 4 deals with the role of social forces in the processes of self-directed learning. The problems involved in dealing with these issues have almost obscured the potential which each set of forces generates for self-directed learning.

Much has been written to illustrate that textbooks, tests, and the other most-used media for teaching could be accurately described as generally racist, ethnocentric, sexist, and middle-class oriented. The situation is improving but all these features remain, to some extent, in the materials used in most schools today. What a number of teachers have done is to teach students to use criteria for analysis of racism, sexism, and other forms of bias and distortion in written material. Students and teachers can then engage cooperatively in rewriting the materials used. In carrying this out, the class learns to use a number of sources of information, to analyze motives, to distinguish between fact and opinion, to draw inferences, and kindred skills. The authors have observed students learning the necessary skills to write their own relatively unbiased material in inner-city schools, suburban schools, and rural areas beginning with fifth- and sixth-grade classes. It may be possible to do this at earlier grade levels as well.

A classroom which has diversity in race, ethnicity, social class, and in representation of sexes can be more productive educationally than a homogeneous one. It lends itself to cooperatively examining values, learning styles, modes of communicating ideas, providing sources of information, and establishing goals, to name just a few examples. The students themselves can act as resources to each other; the greater the diversity, the richer the resources. It is also true that diversity can provide additional bases for conflict and confrontation in the classroom, but that likelihood is lessened if the teachers truly believe that a heterogeneous mix is primarily positive in nature. See Chapter 4 for a more extended treatment of these issues.

I. Students as Resource People

Cross-age tutoring is a relatively new term in education, first appearing in educational literature in the 1950's. Peggy Lippitt and others (1971) conducted research on its use and found the practice to be effective.

Cross-age tutoring typically consists of students being trained to act as tutors to other students who are younger. Those who remember the one-room, multi-grade, country schoolroom (which was common until World War II) will recall that the older students in the higher grades often helped younger students in lower grades in the same classroom. This was often encouraged by the teachers. Its effectiveness is facilitated if no onus is attached to receiving help, if the tutor is not perceived as being "teacher's pet," and if specific training is given in tutoring. Some educators and parents have expressed concern that the tutor is using time that should be devoted to the tutor's own learning and/or that the tutor is doing the teacher's job. Interestingly, research indicates that the act of tutoring is beneficial to learning for the tutor as well as for the recipient of the tutoring.

In self-directed learning the use of cross-age tutoring can be beneficial in several ways. Almost anyone is capable of being a tutor to someone at some time: a person below average in 8th grade arithmetic, for example, may well be able to help an average 5th grade student. Each student needs to learn how to help others, must feel capable of helping others, and actually experience helping others. Additionally, every person needs help at various times, must recognize when it is needed, and be able to ask for it. Above all, students who recognize that they can help each other, learn to do so, and are willing to do so expand their opportunities for learning greatly. The teacher need not be the only source for learning. It is a waste of student talent, as well as an unnecessary burden on teachers, to have just one teacher in a room when there are 25-35 capable, potential teachers.

An added dimension in a classroom which favors self-directed learning would be to have students find out what learning styles are used by other students in the class and to discover styles which might be used or adapted for use by them for their own learning tasks. Not enough evidence is available to judge whether people are capable of only one learning style for most learning tasks or whether it is desirable and possible to learn several styles for use with differing tasks.

J. Promising Practices

A number of promising practices have been cited or described briefly in this chapter. The members of the ASCD Project on Self-Directed Learning plan to compile a list of current examples of promising practices in self-directed learning from different parts of the country for grades K-12. This list will be made available to interested individuals and organizations.

Pat Knudsen, an elementary school principal in Waterford School District, Michigan, has submitted a brief description of highlights of practices in her school which serves as one example of the kinds of information which the proposed written collection of practices will include. Excerpts from her material follow:

If students are to learn to think for themselves, solve problems, and make decisions, they must be allowed to do so. If they are to learn to regulate their lives in accordance with realistic aims and goals, they must be involved in goal-setting. If they are to learn to work effectively with other people, they must have the opportunity to work with others in cooperative problem-solving, decision-making, and goal-setting activities. If they are to develop responsibility, they must be given some freedom to act on their own decisions, but held accountable for and helped to examine the consequences of their actions. If they are to develop self-confidence and self-esteem, they must experience success in self-initiated activities.

Preparation

Preparing children for the important decisions that goal-setting involves takes time. A teacher first sets an atmosphere within the room that is comfortable for discussion. Youngsters are involved in practical experiences designed to increase their awareness of their own feelings, ideas, and beliefs so that their choices and decisions are made on their own values. These experiences are in written forms, such as private journals, or in small group and total group discussions. The main objective is to help children decide what is important to them in evaluating their interests and helping them choose what is important to learn during the school year.

Goal Setting

After children have been prepared for decision making, they choose three or four goals for the school year. These goals can be cognitive, affective, or psychomotor in nature. The children are encouraged to make decisions according to their interests. The goals do not have to fit the current curriculum. The decision is the child's; the staff's job is to provide the learner the opportunity to achieve the goals.

Teacher-Child Conferences

After the child has decided on a goal, he/she has a conference with the teacher. At this conference the child shares his/her goals with the teacher and tells why they are important. The teacher tries to help the child narrow the goal to a specific interest area rather than a general area. (For example, an art goal might be narrowed to specific skills such as drawing or painting.) The teacher and child also discuss ways to accomplish the goals. The child offers suggestions and states the amount of time needed to devote to each goal. At the end of the conference the child's goals are written down. One copy remains for school records and one for the child to take home to share with parents.

Parent-Teacher-Child Conferences

After the first conference, the child is encouraged to share his/her goals with parents. Parents, teacher, and child then have a conference together. Decisions are made as to when the child's goals would be worked on and what each participant in the conference will be responsible for. For example, if a child had the goal to learn to cook, the teacher may assume the responsibility for teaching the child how to measure and to read recipes. The child may be responsible for planning a meal, gathering the necessary ingredients, and following through with the cooking project and the clean up.

The parent would also assume responsibility by agreeing to supply the necessary ingredients and allowing the child to cook at home for instance. At the end of the conference each person—the parent, child, and teacher—has a responsibility to help make each goal a success.

Final Conference

At the end of the year the teacher and child have a conference and discuss each goal. The child discusses feelings of accomplishment or, at times, lack of success. Each child then writes a final evaluation of personal goals. For example: six year old, "I think making goals for myself has been nice. Why? I've been doing better." Fifth grader, "I was successful with this goal. I would have chosen something harder if I had not been having so much trouble with division." Sixth grader, "It didn't take very long for me to reach my goal. I tried not to yell. I tried to keep my mouth closed. . . . I tried not to yell outside but when you are in a championship hockey game and a player misses a breakaway, you try to help him out and you yell and look mad—that will get him mad." Fourth grader, "I can read aloud without being afraid. I was successful. I can read to anyone who asks me. I will never need to have this goal again."

Comments

When educators give students the opportunity to participate in planning their education, they are helping develop decision makers. Students accept the responsibility because they had input. Their ideas and thoughts are respected by their teachers. Teachers, students, and parents work together in helping students become successful. The learning environment helps to encourage independent thinking and creative individuals.

We think our program's emphasis is reflected in this quotation:

I cannot learn to decide
If you make my decision
If you tell me
What to be.
Let me choose what
I must learn.

It is necessary for the future growth of children that they be allowed to make decisions and take on responsibility. They need to conceive of themselves as active agents in their own learning and growth, experiencing the outcome and integrating the fruits and consequences of their choices.

In Conclusion

The material in this chapter indicates a direction for educational change that has been taking place for at least 50 years. The changes are ones in which teachers (or the schools as an institution) move from making all decisions for learners to decision making that is cooperative, with active involvement of students. All teachers have some discretionary authority which they can exercise in their classrooms. It may be as simple as deciding when to study a particular chapter in a textbook or asking what else students would like to know beyond what is required of them. It could be as complex as having students as equal partners in deciding on goals, subject matter, methods of teaching, and evaluation of achievement. It may even extend to having students take the leadership in these areas.

Whether simple or complex in nature, the important principle to keep in mind is that *individual* educators can foster student participation in decision making, whether or not education as a whole moves in that direction. It is easier when others are going in the same direction. But it is not impossible to go against the tide, as the thousands who have done so for years can readily testify.

References

Wilford M. Aikin. *The Story of the Eight Year Study*. New York: Harper and Row, 1942.

William Alexander, Vincent Hines, *et al. Independent Study in Secondary Schools*. New York: Holt, Rinehart, and Winston, 1967.

Alfred Alschuler *et al.* "Social Literacy: A Discipline Game Without Losers." *Phi Delta Kappan* 5(8):606-609; April 1977. There is also a Social Literacy Project at 456 Hills South, University of Massachusetts, Amherst, MA 01002.

Alfred Alschuler, D. Tabor, J. McIntyre. *Teaching Achievement Motivation*. Middletown, Connecticut: Education Ventures, Inc., and Cambridge, Massachusetts: Behavioral Science Center, 1970.

Samuel Baskin. *Quest for Quality: Some Models and Means*. Washington, D.C.: U.S. Office of Education, 1960.

David Beggs and Edward Buffie, editors. *Independent Study*. Bloomington: Indiana University Press, 1957.

Jeanne S. Chall and Allan F. Mersky, editors. *Education and the Brain*. Seventy-seventh Yearbook of the National Society for the Study of Education, Part II. Chicago: University of Chicago Press, 1978.

Patricia Cross. *Accent on Learning*. San Francisco: Jossey-Bass, 1976. pp. 111-33.

Rita Dunn and Kenneth Dunn. *Educator's Self-Teaching Guide to Individualizing Instructional Programs*. New York: Parker Publishing Co., Inc., 1972.

Bernice Felder. "Characteristics of Independent Study Practices in Colleges and Universities of the United States." Unpublished doctoral dissertation, The University of Texas, Austin. *Dissertation Abstracts* 24(7):2807-08: 1964.

Jacob Getzels and Philip W. Jackson. *Creativity and Intelligence*. New York: John Wiley & Sons, 1962.

Miriam L. Goldberg, A. Harry Passow, and Joseph Justman. *The Effects of Ability Grouping*. New York: Teachers College Press, 1966.

Anthony Gregorc. "A New Definition for Individual." *NASSP Bulletin*, February 1977, pp. 20-26.

Anthony Gregorc. *How Learning Style Affects Personal Growth*. Paper presented at Windsor Public Schools, Connecticut, January 27, 1978.

J. P. Guilford. *The Nature of Human Intelligence.* New York: McGraw-Hill Book Company, 1967. pp. 213-14. In popular terms convergent thinking is associated with conformist behavior and divergent thinking is associated with creative behavior.

Joseph E. Hill. *The Educational Sciences.* Revised edition. Bloomfield Hills, Michigan: Oakland Community College, 1976.

David E. Hunt. "Learning Styles and Teaching Strategies." Paper presented at National Council for the Social Studies, Boston, Massachusetts, November 21, 1972. Available from author at OISE, 252 Bloor St. West, Toronto 5, Ontario, Canada.

Bruce Joyce and Marsha Weil. *Models of Teaching.* Englewood Cliffs, New Jersey: Prentice-Hall, Inc., 1972.

Jerome Kagan. In: Irving L. Janis, editor. *Personality Development.* New York: Harcourt Brace Jovanovich, 1971.

Jerome Kagan and John Wright. *Basic Cognitive Processes in Children.* Lafayette, Indiana: Child Development Publications, 1963.

David Kolb *et al. Organizational Psychology: An Experimental Approach.* Englewood Cliffs, New Jersey: Prentice-Hall, Inc., 1971.

David Kolb and Ralph Schwitzgebel. *Changing Human Behavior: Principles of Planned Intervention.* New York: McGraw-Hill Book Company, 1974.

Lawrence Kohlberg. "Education for Justice." In: *Moral Education.* Cambridge, Massachusetts: Harvard University Press, 1970. pp. 57-65.

Peggy Lippitt, R. Lippitt, and J. Eiseman. *Cross-Age Helping Program.* Ann Arbor, Michigan: Center for Research on the Utilization of Scientific Knowledge, 1971.

Mary Nacol Meeker. *The Structure of the Intellect: Its Interpretation and Uses.* Columbus, Ohio: Charles E. Merrill, 1969.

National Association of Secondary School Principals. *Twenty-Five Action Learning Schools.* Reston, Virginia: NASSP, 1974.

National Commission on Resources for Youth. *New Roles for Youth in the School and Community.* New York: Citation Press, 1974.

National Council for the Social Studies. *Education for Democratic Citizenship.* Twenty-second Yearbook. Ryland W. Crary, editor. Washington, D.C.: NCSS, 1951. 161 pp.

National Council for the Social Studies. *Citizenship and a Free Society: Education for the Future.* Thirtieth Yearbook. Franklin Patterson, editor. Washington, D.C.: NCSS, 1960. 292 pp.

National Education Association. *Learning the Ways of Democracy: A Case Book of Civic Education.* Washington, D.C.: NEA, 1940. 486 pp.

NEA Research Bulletin on Ability Grouping 47(3):74-76; October 1968.

W. R. Ogden and P. M. Brewster. "An Analysis of Cognitive Style Profiles and Related Science Achievement Among Secondary Students." ERIC ED 139 610, 1977.

Ralph Ojemann. *Developing a Program for Education in Human Behavior.* Cleveland, Ohio: Educational Research Council of America, 1970.

Louise Parrish and Yvonne Waskin. *Teacher-Pupil Planning for Better Classroom Learning.* New York: Harper & Brothers, 1958.

William T. Plunkett. "An Alternative Approach to Career Education." *Phi Delta Kappan* 56: 628-29: May 1975.

Gerard A. Poirier. *Students as Partners in Team Learning.* Berkeley, California: Center for Team Learning. 1970.

Carl R. Rogers. *Freedom to Learn.* Columbus, Ohio: Charles E. Merrill, 1969.

Marshall Rosenberg. *Diagnostic Teaching.* Washington, D.C.: Special Child Publications, 1968.

Bob Samples. *The Metaphoric Mind.* Reading, Massachusetts: Addison-Wesley, 1976.

Archibald B. Shaw. "The Random Falls Idea." *School Executive*, March 1956. (Whole issue devoted to topic.)

George V. Sheviakov and Fritz Redl. *Discipline for Today's Children and Youth.* Washington, D.C.: Association for Supervision and Curriculum Development, 1944.

Anita Simon and Claudia Byram. *You've Got to Reach'em to Teach'em.* Dallas: TA Press, 1977.

Sidney Simon, L. Howe, and H. Kirschenbaum. *Values Clarification: A Handbook of Practical Strategies for Teachers and Students.* New York: Hart Publishing Co., 1972.

Pamela Smith *et al. Data Bank Guide to Learning Styles: TTP: Mainstreaming Mildly Handicapped Students into the Regular Classroom.* Available from Education Service Center, Region XIII, 6504 Tracor Lane, Austin, TX 78721. (1975.)

Hilda Taba. *The Dynamics of Education.* New York: Harcourt, Brace and Co., 1932.

David A. Thatcher. *Teaching, Loving, and Self-Directed Learning.* Pacific Palisades, California: Goodyear Publishing, 1973.

Herbert Thelen. *Dynamics of Groups at Work.* Chicago: The University of Chicago Press, 1954.

Jan L. Tucker. "Research on Social Studies Teaching and Teacher Education." In: Francis P. Hunkins, editor. *Review of Research in Social Studies Education: 1970-75.* Bulletin 49. Arlington, Virginia: National Council for the Social Studies, 1977. pp. 106-111.

Ralph W. Tyler, editor. *From Youth to Constructive Adult Life: The Role of the School.* Berkeley, California: McCutchan Publishing Corp., 1978.

Gordon F. Vars, editor. *A Bibliography of Research on the Effectiveness of Block-Time Programs.* Kent, Ohio: National Association for Core Curriculum, Kent State University, 1970.

Robert A. Weisgerber. *Perspectives in Individualized Learning.* Chicago: Peacock Publishers, Inc., 1971.

James D. Wells. "Independent Study." In: Gordon Vars, editor. *Common Learnings: Core and Interdisciplinary Team Approaches.* Scranton, Pennsylvania: International Textbook, 1969.

James D. Wells. *Independent Study Students in Secondary Schools and Their Expectations and Satisfactions in Independent Study.* Unpublished doctoral dissertation, University of Florida, Gainesville, 1966. pp. 37-38.

R. K. White and R. Lippitt. *Autocracy and Democracy: An Experimental Inquiry.* New York: Harper & Row, 1960. (Studies carried out in late 1930's.)

H. A. Witkin *et al. Personality Through Perception.* New York: Harper and Brothers, 1954.

Grace S. Wright. *The Core Program: Unpublished Research, 1956-62.* U.S. Office of Education Circular 713. Washington, D.C.: U.S. Government Printing Office, 1963.

Rosalind Zapf. *Democratic Processes in the Secondary Classroom.* Englewood Cliffs, New Jersey: Prentice-Hall, 1959.

3.
Needed Research and Educational Development Work

General Needs

Before dealing with specific needs in research and development work which would improve practices and programs for self-directed learning, several generalizations will be repeated which emerge from the material in the previous chapters:

1. There is a strong base of research data already in evidence to provide solid support for the kinds of self-directed learning which this publication advocates.

2. Successful programs and practices in all aspects of self-directed learning have been observed in every kind of classroom in various parts of the country over the same period of time. The research and practices extend over a period of 40-50 years.

3. Both research and practice give as much support to the value of self-directed learning programs as they do to conventional teacher-directed learning programs, when measures of academic achievement are used.

4. Not only do programs for self-directed learning result in academic achievement comparable to teacher-directed programs, other (additional) objectives in such programs help promote the unique purposes of American education.

Why have self-directed learning programs not become more widespread? Despite the strong evidence to support the fact that students can learn to become self-directed and self-responsible, only a small proportion of schools and classrooms in the country make use of the programs and practices. As a matter of fact, legislatures, school boards, some segments of the public, and some members of the education profession are pushing harder than ever to have student learning controlled, directed, and monitored by adults.

Need for Educational Research in All Areas

One reason for the persistence of conventional programs has to do with money available for research and innovation. Much more money must be allocated for educational research, for development of research into usable classroom practices, for dissemination of promising practices, and for training of educators to upgrade their own knowledge and skills for teaching. This may seem like a foolhardy statement in light of currently strong taxpayer resistance to increased taxes and to other public expenditures. Although precise information is not readily available, it is estimated that business and industry in general spend an average of six percent of operating funds for research, development, and employee training; that growth industries spend ten to fifteen percent of their operating funds for such purposes; and that public education in all sectors probably expends less than one percent of operating funds for comparable purposes. Is it not incongruous that each school district or other education agency can spend several hundred thousand to several hundred million dollars annually for operation without spending the money necessary to find out what it is doing, how well it is doing, what is working (and why), or what is not working (and why not)? Further, the research that has been done and cited previously is rarely an integral part of the operation of an ongoing agency; in most cases the research comes from persons outside the institution being studied.

Each school agency (school district, college, university, intermediate office, state department of education, or other) should have or be part of a system for upgrading its efforts. Such a system would include the components in Figure 1.

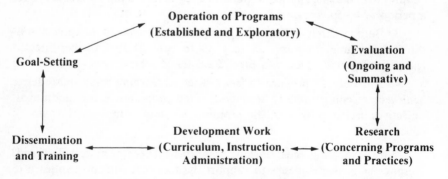

Figure 1. Components of School Agency Upgrading Efforts

Figure 1 illustrates the need for not only carrying on operation of programs, which every agency does, but also the need to: (1) systematically establish and review goals, (2) gather evaluative data on achievement of goals,

(3) carry out operational research concerning programs and practices, (4) conduct development work in curriculum, instruction, and administration in order to translate its research findings into more effective practices in the agency, (5) provide for needed dissemination of innovative ideas, research findings, and evaluation results and training of all personnel, as needed, to carry out new programs/practices. Many school agencies are too small to operate the whole system adequately as depicted here. In those cases, combinations of agencies are needed.

Most education agencies have goal statements of some kind and there is usually an attempt to have those goals reflected in programs and practices. Some ongoing (formative) evaluation takes place: this is the kind that can be used by teachers, students, and others to alter what is going on while it is in progress. Summative evaluation usually takes the form of standardized tests or, increasingly, observation of performance of a narrowly defined competence. Further, most evaluation in schools has to do with accomplishment of the specific practices rather than the attainment of the basic goal. For example, in measuring the ability to write, schools are more likely to concentrate on knowledge of mechanics of grammar instead of the wide array of skills that singly, and in combination, constitute the ability to write. In areas such as scientific problem-solving ability or citizenship development there is even greater likelihood that evaluation will be concerned with recall of facts and simple elements of inference rather than with the kinds of decision-making skills which are part of our daily lives or scientific endeavors.

Simply stated, there are few examples of districts or colleges and universities which carry out research concerning their own programs and practices and fewer still in which the work necessary to develop evaluation and research findings for use in the school or classroom is in evidence. Of the two remaining components, there is some evidence of increased use of agency-sponsored in-service education and curriculum development as well as use of external dissemination systems, like ERIC. However, even in these activities the training (in-service education) and curriculum development are rarely based on any evaluation data or research data from the agency itself; that is, they are rarely designed to capitalize on what has been found to work well or to overcome any gaps or weaknesses discovered through systematic rational analysis. Obviously if there is no comprehensive evaluation or any research and development activity within that system, it is not possible to base in-service education activities or curriculum development activities on either research or evaluation findings.

A concluding note on the components proposed for upgrading education is to call attention to the need for exploratory programs and practices. High morale and enthusiasm are often engendered by the opportunity to try out new ideas simply because they are exciting to the person(s) involved. It is deadly to creative people to be part of a bureaucracy which requires that all activities fit the system before they can be explored. Quite often we do not know what an idea means, what its purposes are, or what its value might be until we try to put it into operation.

In the field of education there has been some recognition of the need for research, for development work, and for dissemination of promising practices. National legislation has created research and development centers, regional development laboratories, and various information retrieval and dissemination systems. The major flaw in this approach is that each of these agencies is an autonomous entity with its own goals, program, and practices. Education needs regional and national agencies to do this work but they should complement or supplement basic activities of the same nature carried on by the home agency or institution.

Every school district and other educational agency should spend an amount equal to at least five percent of its operating budget both to ensure that the money already used for operation is being spent wisely and also to provide for needed upgrading of people, programs, and practices. This has been demonstrated to be of benefit wherever such monies were allocated. Until something approaching this is done, changes in education will continue to be based largely on whim, expediency, uninformed popular opinion, and power politics.

Specific Needs for Research and Development Work

A number of questions should be explored in order to improve the state of the art of self-directed teaching. Additionally, those promising activities already identified should be publicized and used more widely. Among the questions worthy of study or further research:

• How can students develop a variety of learning styles which they then learn to apply approximately to given tasks? While some attention has been given to identifying the learning style used or preferred by each student, little has been done to determine if it is possible and desirable for individual students to develop an array of styles to choose among.

• Are there particular learning styles which uniquely fit each student and will develop for that student under certain conditions? It appears to be so but, if true, under what conditions?

• To what extent can teachers understand, appreciate, and accept students who have learning styles different from the teacher? Do teachers have blind spots in this regard? (Compare Kohlberg's idea that people at different levels of moral development may not be able to understand each other.)

• How can cognitive mapping concepts (Hill, 1976) be developed into usable practices? Initial development work has taken place (see Chapter 2) but is limited in scope at the moment.

• How can research data on the "other-half" of the brain and Guilford's (1962) concept of 120 different intellectual processes be developed further for use in schools?

• The ideas developed for use of split-brain research in the classroom (Samples, 1976) and for classroom implications of J. P. Guilford's work (Meeker, 1969) should be tried out by many educators in different settings and with different age groups. Continuation of research reviewed in the 1978 NSSE Yearbook, *Education and the Brain* (Chall, 1978), is also needed and exciting to contemplate.

• Is there an age at which "imprinting" takes place for learning styles and beyond which time, little change can take place? If so, at what age or stage of development does this occur? There is need to correlate the work of developmentalists Piaget, Erikson, and Havighurst with recent findings about the nature of the brain in an attempt to answer these questions.

• What kinds of child-rearing practices assist in stimulating creative thinking and divergent thinking? Some information is now available on this score. How can it be developed for use with and by parents?

• What can parents do for children at various ages to help increase their children's ways of learning to be self-directed? What should schools do to help without intruding on proper parental prerogatives?

• Are there identifiable stages of each child's development for learning how to carry out each of the various aspects of self-directed learning, such as individual goal-setting and group goal-setting? If so, what are they? What methods can be used by teachers, administrators, and others so that what is expected of particular individuals and specific age-groups of students is realistic and reasonable?

• How can students be taught to recognize what their own learning styles are? How can they learn to deal with other people's styles in ways that complement or otherwise support each other? How do students learn to cope with apparently conflicting styles of teacher-student and student-student?

• To what extent are the differences in learning styles associated with a person's sex determined by inheritance and to what extent by the culture? How do teachers and the students take sex-related differences into account for the mutual benefit of both sexes?

• Are there real differences in learning styles which are due to race, ethnic background, or social class? If so, what is their nature? How do they promote or inhibit self-directed or self-responsible learning? If these differences do exist, how can self-directed learning be fostered in a manner not dominated by the majority group viewpoint?

• Does learning improve when teacher and students are grouped according to compatibility of teaching style and learning styles, as Herbert Thelen has suggested?

• To what extent is learning enhanced when there is diversity of learning styles in a classroom, particularly if students are identifying and trying out various learning styles?

• Which of the techniques used by teachers to diagnose learning problems and prescribe educational activities for students can be taught to students and used successfully by them? At what ages and in what forms?

• It would be helpful to conduct research studies of classroom climate (authoritarian, democratic, and laissez-faire) at different grade levels—not so much to determine which is better but to gain insight about the dynamics of the forces at work under these differing climates as they affect all major goals of education. Goals related to traditional academic achievement may be affected differently than those related to decision making and to planning, for example, for each of the three climates.

• An updated version of the Eight Year Study (Aikin, 1942) would also be interesting and productive. One criticism of this study is the experimenter effect which yields favorable results due to enthusiasm of participants in trying out new approaches and in being in the limelight of a study. It would be interesting to use the results of the Eight Year Study to focus on the elements which might have accounted for students' success in college. To illustrate, the schools departing most from traditional practices, out of the 30 schools involved, seemed to produce the highest achievement levels in student leadership as well as in academic learning. To which feature, or combination of features, was this attributable? Was it due to integration of subject fields, to the extent of teacher-pupil planning, to the focus on problem-solving skills, to some combination of the foregoing, or to something else?

• The effects of a curriculum based on developmental tasks of life rather than traditional subject matter should be tried out at all grade levels for all the required, general education parts of the curriculum. This idea was part of the approach used in some schools of the Eight Year Study and a number of elementary schools have tried to organize teaching units around common life tasks over the course of the past 30-40 years. There is no comprehensive, long-term research on its strengths and shortcomings, however. If this research were to be conducted, the traditional academic subject fields of reading, science, arithmetic, writing, social studies, and English would give way to studies of how to cope with tasks confronting people at various stages/ages of development. All the basic general education knowledge and skills now encompassed in the familiar subject fields would still be studied, not as separately taught subjects but as needed to deal with the life tasks (Havighurst, 1951).

• The long-term effects of current programs for individualizing instruction should be investigated. How do the many varieties of individually prescribed instruction and alternative forms of programmed instruction affect attitudes of self-responsibility and the skills needed for becoming self-directed? Are we actually producing greater academic achievement through these approaches? Whether or not more academic learning results, are we also fostering dependency and developing robot-like citizens in the process?

• What can schools do to help parents understand and accept the learning styles their children use, if those styles are significantly different from those favored by the parents?

Needed Dissemination Work

A number of promising practices from the past and present should be publicized and opportunity provided for more teachers to learn how to use them. Some of the most promising include:

• The unified studies and core curriculum approaches in secondary schools and the unit and project approaches in elementary schools may be "old" ideas to experienced people in the profession, but they are unfamiliar to most newcomers.

Edwin White furnishes some material about an interdisciplinary, problem-solving approach in elementary school education referred to as the Unified Science and Mathematics for Elementary Schools (USMES). Funded since 1970 by the National Science Foundation, "The USMES program attempts to develop problem-solving abilities by having students work on the actual problems they encountered in their school and community environment" (Lomon, 1975). *The USMES Guide* (Education Development Center, 1976), a *USMES Teacher Resource Book: Ways to Learn/Teach* (Education Development Center, 1975), and an article by White (1978) provide excellent descriptions for anyone wishing to explore the work.

• Community school and community-based educational programs in which parent education programs complement school-directed activities should be expanded—particularly programs designed to help children be more open to new ideas, to new activities, and to new ways of solving problems.

The Mott Foundation is now helping provide funding for certain kinds of community school programs. It is also true that state and federal governments have provided sanctions for community involvement in schools generally. This is not necessarily community-based education. Community-based education has at least three distinctive features: the community comes into the school and classrooms, the school goes out into the community, and schools give major attention to improving the quality of life now in the community through joint efforts with other community agencies in ongoing community activities.

• Values clarification exercises (Simon *et al.*), moral education techniques (Kohlberg), and Ojemann's "causal" teaching approaches should be used in different combinations and modified to suit the setting. New and better approaches will evolve out of this.

• The work begun by Alschuler and others (1970) in teaching achievement motivation should be extended to many more locations. Additionally, the practices should be adapted for use in the upper elementary grades and, perhaps, the lower elementary grades as well.

• The use of ability groups for general education purposes should be replaced by heterogeneous grouping for class sections. Reasons for this have already been described in the previous chapter. The use of ability groups within class, as one of many forms of grouping used to meet different goals, is probably justified. Research evidence supports heterogeneous grouping and some studies support interest grouping or friendship grouping but the major finding is that the form of grouping used should be directly related to the purposes sought and to the methods, activities, and materials to be used (Wayne County).

• College-preparatory tracks should be abolished in favor of functional individualized curricula. Many high schools have moved in this direction but the college-prep curriculum still persists and, in many places, predominates. The common needs of college-bound students are general life skills and knowledge—needs they share with all other students, including those not going on to college.

General life skills courses in science, to name one area, would not be junior versions of college chemistry and college physics but consumer-oriented science courses designed to help all citizens cope with the personal and societal issues science touches on. One of the most damaging effects of the national post-Sputnik hysteria for upgrading science and mathematics was the development of courses in science and mathematics which proportionately fewer students take each year. "New science" and "new math" may be great for potential scientists and mathematicians but are seen as irrelevant by most other students.

Our schools need to provide enough understanding of science and mathematics, particularly statistics, environmental education, and computer sciences, so that citizens can participate in making intelligent decisions about allocation and use of material resources.

If curriculum tracks are abolished, they would be replaced by a set of courses or experiences required of all, and other courses available for exploration of interests and for pursuit of careers or other specialized needs and interests. This can take many forms.

• Increasingly, students should help each other learn. The skills needed in order to have students learn from each other are relatively easily learned.

Benefits can accrue to teachers and students through more widespread use of what is now referred to as cross-age tutoring, by use of small planning groups, by fostering paired-learning, by use of learning teams, and by teacher-pupil planning. The teacher must spend some time in determining which of these approaches is appropriate to use for particular purposes, followed by explanation of what is to be done. The most difficult part of instituting these practices, for a teacher who has not previously engaged students in learning how to help each other, is to overcome the attitudes of competition and negative reaction to cooperation which students have experienced previously in school.

• Self-directed learning programs can represent one effective way to mainstream exceptional students. The elements of self-directed learning stress individualizing one's own education with the active assistance of the teacher and others who are part of the learning situation. Public law 94-142 calls for learning in "the least restrictive environment" (mainstreaming) for students usually labeled as handicapped in some sense.

Whether students are certifiably gifted, handicapped, or "normal," they are most likely to achieve their own potential if they learn how to: (1) discover their values and establish appropriate educational goals, (2) diagnose their own strengths and weaknesses in relation to what they seek to achieve, (3) develop individual plans and plans with others for activities which will lead to goal attainment, (4) learn to identify their own learning style(s) and how to use the style(s) which fits them and the task at hand, (5) identify and use a variety of resources in problem solving, and (6) discover how to assess progress and achievement of goals for themselves and the group of which each is part. Many students can be taught to write their own "individual learning plan" with the teacher instead of having the teacher write it for them.

Concluding Comments

The research and development needs described in this chapter look formidable. A list of research and development needs for traditional education would look equally imposing if compiled in this manner. As in all other fields of human endeavor, the more that is learned, the more we become aware of what we do not yet know. What is encouraging is that a great deal is now known about what does not work, in addition to the useful information from research and practice concerning promising paths to follow. It is possible, therefore, to improve education for self-directed learning simply by abandoning ineffective practices or programs in some cases and by adopting some easily-installed promising practices in other cases. While the current mood in the country and in the profession is for more control and more

48   MOVING TOWARD SELF-DIRECTED LEARNING

direction from the top, each member of the profession has some control over what he or she does. As a consequence, each of us can bring about some change at the place where it counts most after all. That is, we can change what each of us does in the direction we want to go. Students learn to become self-directed when surrounded by self-directed teachers. It certainly helps if parents, administrators, and others also display behaviors which foster movement toward more self-direction in education for all parties involved.

References

Wilford M. Aikin. *The Story of the Eight Year Study*. New York: Harper & Row Publishers, Inc., 1942.

Alfred Alschuler, D. Tabor, and J. McIntyre. *Teaching Achievement Motivation*. Middletown, Connecticut: Education Ventures, Inc., and Cambridge, Massachusetts: Behavioral Science Center, 1970.

Jeanne S. Chall and Allan F. Mersky, editors. *Education and the Brain*. Seventy-seventh Yearbook of the National Society for the Study of Education, Part II. Chicago: University of Chicago Press, 1978.

Education Development Center. *The USMES Guide*. Newton, Massachusetts: EDC, 1976.

Education Development Center. *USMES Teacher Resource Book: Ways to Learn/Teach*. Newton, Massachusetts: EDC, June 1975.

J. P. Guilford. *The Nature of Human Intelligence*. New York: McGraw-Hill Book Co., 1962. pp. 213-14. In popular terms convergent thinking is associated with conformist behavior and divergent thinking is associated with creative behavior.

Robert J. Havighurst. *Developmental Tasks and Education*. New York: Longmans, Green & Co., 1951.

Joseph B. Hill. *The Educational Sciences*. Revised edition. Bloomfield, Michigan: Oakland Community College, 1976.

Earle L. Lomon et al. "Real Problem-Solving in USMES: Interdisciplinary Education and Much More." *School Science and Mathematics* 75(1); January 1975.

Mary Nacol Meeker. *The Structure of the Intellect: Its Interpretation and Uses*. Columbus, Ohio: Charles E. Merrill, 1969.

Bob Samples. *The Metaphoric Mind*. Reading, Massachusetts: Addison-Wesley, 1976.

Wayne County. A number of unpublished studies comparing ability grouping with groups formed on the basis of interest in the same topics or groups formed on the basis of friendships were carried out by the Wayne County Study of the Gifted and Talented (Michigan) in the 1958-61 time period. No difference in achievement scores was noted in most cases but where they did occur they favored the interest grouping and friendship grouping.

Edwin P. White. "Problem-Solving: Its History as a Focus in Curriculum Development." *School Science and Mathematics* 78(3): 183-88; March 1978.

4.
Social-Cultural Forces Affecting Self-Directed Learning

In preparing this publication, members of ASCD's Project on Self-Directed Learning recognize the major role played by social and cultural forces in teaching and learning. How do these forces specifically affect programs designed to increase self-directed and self-responsible learning?

There is ample evidence to suggest that one's own experiences and racial/ethnic background provide each of us differing insights into the nature of the issues involved. With that in mind, we invited Claire B. Halverson, Alberto Ochoa, Ana Maria Rodriguez, and Barbara Sizemore to share their expert views in these matters with us.

Halverson has worked in the Midwest for more than ten years in inservice education programs designed to overcome institutional racism. Ochoa and Rodriguez are faculty members in the Department of Multicultural Education at San Diego State University. Sizemore was an educator in The Woodlawn Organization (TWO) in the Chicago area, became the first black woman to serve as Superintendent of Schools of the District of Columbia, and is now at the University of Pittsburgh. Their experience, research, knowledge, and commitment to social issues are reflected in the following contributions.

Forces Which Affect Self-Direction
and Self-Responsibility of Students

Barbara A. Sizemore

Many social-cultural forces affect the self-direction and self-responsibility of black students. The most important of these forces is the imputation of black inferiority conferred upon black students giving them unequal status (Greenstone and Peterson, 1973; Sizemore, 1978). Judged by their socially selected physical traits and cultural attributes, black students are frequently placed in unfriendly, unresponsive, and unsupportive educational environments where teachers are negatively oriented, if not openly hostile, to them. Moreover, their attempts at self-direction are thwarted by grouping practices based on ability, reading, or achievement; the age-graded vertical organization of their institutions; and the norm-referenced curriculum emphasizing white, affluent, Anglo-Saxon life experiences.

The problems that black students have generally center on discipline, learning, and self-concept. To alleviate these problems educational strategies compatible with their growth rates, development patterns, learning styles, cultural heritage, and sociolinguistic experiences are needed. However, the curriculum of the American public school is taken from the affluent, white, Anglo-Saxon family's book of life. The experiences of others are often absent or briefly appended. The nuclear WASP family includes Mother, Father, Sister, Brother, dog, and cat. They live in a little white house with a triangular roof surrounded by a green yard and a white picket fence. Too often black students neither identify with this family or recognize its values and norms. Consequently, the already-developed systems of self-direction and self-responsibility operating in the black community of high rise apartments are unacceptable in the American public school classroom. In many situations, these systems involve: (1) the care of younger siblings; (2) the execution of family responsibilities (marketing, paying bills, receiving goods and services); (3) the protection of self from hostile neighbors and peers; and (4) the preservation of family values, (appreciation for black history, black heroes and heroines, and black institutions).

Unfortunately, the public school does not reinforce these experiences. The norms of the public school emerge from the WASP gestalt, and teaching strategies are designed to enlarge this life style. Curriculum content and methodology are constructed to develop the WASP child's potential while the black child's definitions, assessment, and explanations of appropriate institutional behavior are irrelevant. Consequently, this denial of recognition and respect forces black students to seek alternative goals for self-actualization (Sizemore, 1978; Clark, 1973).

Moreover, black students seem to learn better when cognitive tasks are related to psychomotor activities. Harry Morgan explains this relationship in his research. He says that many ". . . black people have a cognitive style which seems to require a more active interaction with the learning environment than what is needed by their white counterparts. Top performance demands a compatible interaction between cognitive (information processing) and the motoric (physical output) domains with circular reinforcement from one domain to the other" (Morgan, 1977).

The passive, sedentary environment of the American public school is disadvantageous to black students who must be aggressively involved in the learning activity. Black students seem to need to act, to be engaged, to be doing while learning. Teachers need to understand how to present procedural knowledge concerned with teaching the learner how to do something. Most teachers understand only propositional knowledge or content concerned with knowing *that* or knowing *what* (Olson, 1973).

Another difference between black and white students is their language usage. Black students speak a dialect called "Black English." Although many black teachers and educators disavow it, most black students speak it. Smitherman (1977) posits that certain characteristics of Black English could be used to teach black students Standard English. She says that teachers need to learn how to use what the kids already know to move them to what they need to know. Smitherman finds:

[If] you genuinely accept as viable the language and culture the child has acquired by the time he or she comes to school . . . it follows that you allow the child to use the language to express himself or herself, not only to interact with the peers in the classroom but with you, the teachers as well . . . (1977).

She urges educators to use the "call-response" dynamic integral to the communication system of Black English in an interactive way to facilitate learning for those black students who cannot learn in a passive way. "Call-response" involves a leader who "calls" the message to be disseminated and the respondent who "delivers" the response. Teachers then include the learner in the process in an active way. Other techniques which Smitherman advocates are peer group tutoring, rhymes and rhyming patterns, and tonal semantics.

Black students have other strengths such as interests and, sometimes, skills in music and art. The ability to reproduce sounds on musical instruments or with the voice should be used in ways to facilitate learning the other symbol systems, that is, numbers and words. The ability to reproduce images is related to the ability to articulate thoughts in words. Additionally, music and art involve action and psychomotor activities.

The lives of black children from large, poor families dictate an extraordinarily different repertoire of experiences in self-direction and self-responsibility. They may not need two or three weeks of learning sharing; they may need to learn ownership. They may not need to "play house"; but instead may need to start cognitive development skills immediately. They may not need to learn to count; they may need to learn the meaning of the number one. They may not need to learn their ABC's; they may need to learn the sounds of those letters. Indeed, teaching the ABC's may increase their difficulty in learning those sounds.

To teach self-reliance, President Julius Nyerere of Tanzania says that education should prepare young people to live in and to serve society. But, a decision must be made first about what kind of society is to be built. In Tanzania, the polity wants a society based on: equality and respect for human dignity; sharing of the resources produced by the efforts of all; work by everyone, exploitation by none. This means that the educational system will stress cooperative endeavors as opposed to competitive individual efforts. It will stress service as opposed to profit and will counteract the tendency to develop an intellectual elite tempted to despise those who have no special academic abilities. Obviously, this kind of self-direction and self-responsibility would not serve the competitive, profit-making social order in the United States.

In order for a self-directed, self-responsible black youth to emerge from the present social order, changes in the passive, sedentary teaching-learning environment have to occur. The docile, black learner who quietly acquiesces, complies, and conforms to social arrangements which confirm his/her subordinate role may not learn as easily or may not learn at all. Accordingly, such a student exacerbates his/her unequal racial status.

Both Freire (1971, 1973) and Woodson (1933) oppose the banking-deposit system of teaching wherein the student is regarded as an object. Woodson wrote that the purpose of education was to inspire people to live more abundantly, to learn to begin with life as they found it and make it better. The mere imparting of information was not education to him; for the goal of education was to make people think and do for themselves (Sizemore, 1973).

Freire advocates a problem-posing cognitive approach which will deepen our consciousness about our situation enabling us to apprehend it as historical reality susceptible of transformation, and to act thereupon. For him the dialogue was the center of his curriculum, beginning with the word itself which had two elements: reflection and action. For Freire, dialogue was the encounter between people, mediated by the world in order to name that world. Self-direction and self-responsibility for black youth depend on the ability to order that world by using their own sociolinguistic experiences, life realities, growth rates, and development patterns in a teaching-learning environment, free from the imputation of black inferiority, where they enjoy equal status.

Individual and Cultural Determinants of Self-Directed Learning Ability: Straddling an Instructional Dilemma

Claire Halverson

Are there conditions of race/ethnicity or sex which affect one's ability to be a self-directed and self-responsible learner? Traditionally there have been group as well as individual differences in achievement as measured by standardized tests in the public schools. Racial/ethnic minority students (blacks, Hispanics, and Native Americans) have not achieved as well on these tests as white, middle-class students.

In addition, there are achievement differences in male and female students. Girls do well in the primary grades but clearly slip behind starting at junior high. There are also differences in types of achievement; females do better in verbal areas such as language arts, while males are more proficient in spatial, analytic areas such as math and science.

The urban education literature of the 1960's is saturated with explanations of low achievement of racial/ethnic minorities and low income students. These children were seen as "culturally disadvantaged" or "deprived" which was supposed to explain their low achievement. This is seen increasingly as blaming the victim instead of the cause.

More current explanations of low achievement of these groups refer to institutional racism and school-related causes such as low teacher and counselor expectations and behavior which does not hold these students to standards or which holds male and female students to differentiated standards; inability of schools to relate positively to parents of racial/ethnic minority students; and curriculum materials, instructional practices, and school organizational patterns which favor white, middle-class students and contribute to differentiated outcomes for male and female students.

Learning Style in Relation to Group Differential Achievement

One possible cause of low achievement among racial/ethnic minorities and differentiated achievement between males and females which has received minimal attention is the possibility of differentiated sex and racial/ethnic learning styles. The focus on individual differences in the last decade has produced data on the existence of, and systems of identifying, individual differences in learning styles, particularly cognitive style. This research has focused on "global-analytic capacity" (Davis and Klausmeier, 1970; Ohnmacht, 1966) and more total "cognitive mapping" incorporating symbolic orientation, cultural influences, and modalities inference (Hill,

1974). Family background, talent, life experiences, and personal goals influence these learning styles, it is felt. Little concern has been shown for cultural group differences in addition to individual differences. Is this because group deviation from the white, Anglo-Saxon Protestant male, a minority to be sure but one on which our cultural standards are based, has always been seen as negative? Is this because differences have been explained as genetic rather than cultural as in "women's intuition" or the "natural rhythm" of blacks? Is this because discussion of group differences has led to stereotyping instead of recognizing patterns? If schools are designed to encourage more self-directedness and self-responsibility, learning styles of students must be identified. There will certainly be individual differences in learning style, but there is growing evidence to suggest group differences as well. Although there may be patterns of behavior within a racial/ethnic group, there are intragroup differences based on such characteristics as (1) religion; (2) urban-rural; (3) economic status; (4) length of time in the country (generally third generation members of racial/ethnic groups tend to be assimilated); (5) location in a given part of the country (Mexican-Americans in the Southwest maintain closer ties to Mexico than those who live in the Midwest) and number of the group in the area (racial/ethnic group identity is stronger when there are larger numbers. A Swedish American in the East is not identified; in the Midwest he/she is a "Swede"); (6) visible identity (people of color are easily identified as not being a part of the most acceptable group); (7) level of education; and (8) language used. A Mexican American, for example, who is Catholic, lives in a small town in Texas, has low income, has been in the country less than three generations, and has dark skin and dark hair, will tend to retain a significant part of cultural behavior traditionally found in Mexican American communities.

To what extent are there cultural differences between males and females? Bem (1975), in a study of undergraduates at Stanford University, has found that about 50 percent describe themselves with adjectives which are "appropriate" to their sex role, 15 percent report themselves to be cross-sex typed, and about 35 percent see themselves as having characteristics which are androgynous. Is this self reporting method and college student sample indicative of more general male-female differences? There has been little work in the area, and sex roles are changing. There is even less clarity about the causes of adherence to or deviation from group standards for males and females. Hunsaker (1978), using the instrument developed by Bem which groups personality characteristics into sex appropriate or sex inappropriate categories, found a high level of sex stereotyped expectations in parents of newborn children. Other studies show that parents have different behavioral and career expectations for their babies dressed in blue than their daughters, and that boys are handled more roughly even as babies. Several studies have reported that achievement-oriented behavior in girls, a "male" cultural characteristic, is prevalent among females whose mothers have been "pushy," "not protective," and "less nurturant" (Crandall *et al*, 1964; Kagan and Moss, 1962).

Cultural Learning Styles Chart

If there are cultural as well as individual differences, how do they affect learning styles? The chart that follows, "Cultural Learning Styles," was developed by this author in order to create a structure which would help educators identify cultural patterns relevant to learning styles and suggest classroom instructional strategies. The work by Ramirez, Herold, and Casteneda (1975) in this area has been most helpful in developing categories of the chart. The chart indicates questions about values, beliefs, and behaviors which are relative to learning style in the areas of child-adult relations, child-child relations, and cognitive learning styles; selected cultural patterns of racial/ethnic and sex groups; and suggested classroom instructional strategies.

Data for the documentation of cultural patterns has come from the references following. Cultural patterns for each racial/ethnic and sex group are based on the references and research primarily carried out by members of the group in question. Additionally, once the chart was developed, members of each racial/ethnic and sex group who are familiar with research on cultural differences were consulted to test the validity of the constructs shown.

The five cultural groups are: Low-income Urban Black; Traditional Mexican American; Traditional Native American; Middle-class White; and Traditional Female. These groups were included in the chart because the most relevant research available concerned them. The chart does not attempt to be complete, but, rather, to give selected illustration examples. A complete taxonomy may not be possible at this time due to insufficient available research. Cultural patterns are only briefly described. Their sociological and historical causes cannot be thoroughly analyzed within this brief section, nor can the complexity and variations of the behavior within groups be described. There exist cultural as well as individual differences in learning style, and these have implications for schools in a culturally pluralistic society. For a more thorough understanding of the learning style of any one racial/ethnic or sex group, the reader may wish to read the references cited.

Again, selected patterns are not intended to refer to all members of the group; there are many individual differences within cultural groups. There is still much controversy in the area of cultural differences since these differences even in the 1970's are perceived by some educators to mean inferiority of the oppressed group and all members of the oppressed group are stereotyped into these patterns.

Low-income Urban Black. Billingsley (1969) points out that there are two distinct groups within the low-income black group: the working poor and the non-working poor. Addison (1976) suggests that much of what is called "black culture" is generated from this latter group, and is distinct from other racial/ethnic low-income groups. He also finds similar value constructs among black nationalists. (See also, Foster, 1971).

Traditional Mexican American. Ramirez, Herold, and Casteneda (1975) suggest that traditional core values and behavior are most apt to be found among families that live in communities over which Mexican Americans have a significant measure of control, live near the Mexican border, identify with Mexican Catholic ideology, and live in rural areas.

Traditional Native American. Brewer (n.d.) suggests that even on government reservations, white values and behaviors are superimposed on Native American culture. She believes, however, that basic Native American cultural and value systems remain in operation. Forbes (1973), in discussing goals of education written from a Native American viewpoint, states that general goals can be developed without relating to any specific Native American group. These goals reflect the basic values of Native American societies. Traditional Native American values and behaviors are more prevalent on reservations and among Native Americans in urban areas who are trying to relearn their culture. These values and behaviors are less prevalent generally in urban areas. (See also, Pelletier, n.d.)

Middle-class White. Within the white middle-class two groups begin to appear at adolescence. Those who adhere to traditional values and behaviors and strive to achieve academically and athletically, and those who reject these goals, although in many cases they probably could reasonably well attain them. Patterns for white middle-class listed on the chart refer to the "strivers" or "achievers."

Traditional Female. Bem (1975) found that 50 percent of the female undergraduates who completed a personality characteristics instrument responded in an "appropriate" manner for females, whereas 15 percent responded in an "appropriate" manner for males, and 35 percent were androgynous. (See: Baumrind, 1972; Janis and Field, 1959; Maccoby and Jacklin, 1974; Walker and Heyns, 1962; Witkin *et al.*, 1954.)

Cultural Learning Styles

Questions About Values, Beliefs, and Behavior	Selected Cultural Patterns of Racial/Ethnic and Sex Groups	Suggested Classroom Instructional Strategies
Child-Adult Relations 1. Does the child obey the adult because of his/her role as adult or must respect be earned?	*Low-income Urban Black* Respect is earned by adult relating to child as an individual. Child responds to shame and to avoidance of physical punishment. Child may openly confront adult if respect is not earned.	Teacher needs to earn respect by relating to students personally.
	Traditional Native American Leaders chosen by community and will stay as long as community accepts them. Older adults seen as wise.	Teacher can gain respect if he/she demonstrates acceptable behavior. Older teachers may more easily gain respect.
	Traditional Mexican American Respect is given to adult if adult demonstrates approved values such as contributing to community.	Same as above.
	Middle-class White Respect is earned. Boys allowed more open disagreement; girls not encouraged to be aggressive and disagreement is more passive and hidden. Child responds to guilt, withdrawal of love, and external rewards.	Teacher may need to encourage children away from external rewards such as grades in order to be self-directed.
2. Does the child seek a relationship with the adult which is friendly and personal or formal and task-oriented?	*Traditional Mexican American* Child seeks friendly and personal adult relationships.	Teacher needs to arrange instructional time so that he/she can work with students in a small group and in individualized situations where personal feelings and experiences can be shared. Since assistance to

Questions About Values, Beliefs, and Behaviors	Selected Cultural Patterns of Racial/Ethnic and Sex Groups	Suggested Classroom Instructional Strategies
		others is given freely without asking for it and is highly valued, teacher needs to be sensitive to need for help. Older students also need to experience working in a more formal and task-oriented situation.
	Middle-class White Child functions in relationship which is somewhat formal and task-oriented.	Child can try working independently of teacher; interactions with teacher can focus on task at hand. Child working alone should not be perceived as rejecting teacher or other children.
3. Is the child encouraged to disagree or challenge the adult on ideas or is disagreement seen as disrespectful?	*Traditional Native American* Respect shown to adult does not allow disagreement. Adult perceived as wise, particularly if old.	Teacher should avoid placing student in a position which encourages him/her to disagree. Teacher who perceives self as an equal to students may find student doesn't share that opinion. Student may be unsure how to act in this situation.
	Middle-class White Child is encouraged to challenge adult on opinions.	Teacher can play "devil's advocate" to stimulate independent thinking.
Child-Child Relations 4. How do boys and girls interact with each other?	*Traditional Mexican American* Physical contact and discussion of sex are not sanctioned between adolescent boys and girls.	Human relations and physical education activities which encourage physical contact between boys and girls should be avoided so that girls are not placed in a position where school encourages them to violate their self-respect.
5. Does the child work well with children who are older, younger, and/or the same age.	*Low-income Urban Black* Children are frequently partially cared for by older siblings. After	Cross-age tutoring and multi-age classrooms can be used effectively.

Questions About Values, Beliefs, and Behaviors	Selected Cultural Patterns of Racial/Ethnic and Sex Groups	Suggested Classroom Instructional Strategies
	about age six, children relate mostly to peers.	
6. Does the child work well independently or cooperatively with other students?	*Low-income Urban Black and Traditional Mexican American* Children are encouraged to help siblings, particularly younger ones. Families tend to be large and may include cousins. Competition discouraged. Peer groups tend to be strong and give members support.	Small group situations where students cooperate; tutoring and paired learning are encouraged. Where peer groups are strong, it may be helpful to maintain existing peer group as instructional group in classroom. Students may need more practice working by themselves.
	Traditional Native American Individual competition or demonstrating achievement in front of group discouraged. Competition appropriate in sports with teams.	Same as above.
	Middle-class White Male Working independently is highly valued.	Students can learn when working by themselves and may need skill development in working cooperatively.
	Traditional Female Girls are not encouraged to problem-solve independently. Friendliness and ability to get along with others valued, so conflict and disagreement are frequently hidden.	Female students may need skill development in facing independent tasks and in reducing test anxiety.
7. How is status achieved?	*Traditional Mexican American* Working for the benefit of family and community and assisting others are highly valued.	Small group situations where students can cooperate. Tutoring and paired learning are encouraged. If competition with others is used, even those who excel may not want to participate in outshining their peers. Students need practice work-

Questions About Values, Beliefs, and Behaviors	Selected Cultural Patterns of Racial/Ethnic and Sex Groups	Suggested Classroom Instructional Strategies
		ing in competitive situations, such as timed tests, so that they can also do well in these situations.
	Low-income Urban Black Rivalry and competition are discouraged in augmented families and working for benefit of family is emphasized. Status is also given for one's communicative style.	Teacher should avoid embarassing student in front of peers. Direct confrontation better handled privately with students.
	Traditional Native American Person should be developed in many spheres of life including spiritual, bodily, and artistic ability, not only marketable skills. Dignity in front of peers highly valued.	Teacher should develop program to facilitate holistic development.
	Middle-class White Male Achievement and being the best highly valued in academic and athletic areas.	Students will respond to competitive situations where they can excel. If they perceive they cannot compete, they may give up. Relying on competition is questionable since only those who feel comfortable in succeeding may respond. Status for working cooperatively needs to be encouraged.
	Traditional Female Physical appearance and friendliness valued. Academic achievement negatively valued as girls approach adolescence since this is seen as unfeminine, particularly in science and math. Approval from males is often negatively related to academic success.	Female students need to overcome fear of rejection for excellence. They may need opportunities to compete only with other females. They also need to be encouraged to use their abilities when working with male students.

Questions About Values, Beliefs, and Behaviors	Selected Cultural Patterns of Racial/Ethnic and Sex Groups	Suggested Classroom Instructional Strategies
8. Does the student become more involved in the task or social surroundings?	*Traditional Female, Traditional Mexican American, and Low-income Urban Black* Child is sensitive to feelings of others. "Soul" (empathetic understanding), the ability to participate in the feelings of others or the capacity to interject one's own emotions into a situation to be able to analyze subjectively all the nuances of feelings in that situation, is valued among low income urban blacks.	Teacher needs to allow time for students to relate personally to each other before working together; tasks may not be completed successfully unless human relations have been attended to.
Cognitive Style 9. Is the child more analytic or global in problem solving? (*Analytic*: Field independent, gives attention to parts and details; abstract thinking, spatial ability, and analytic problem solving skills; inductive thinking or forming generalizations. *Global*: Field sensitive or field dependent, gives attention to whole contextual field; holistic thinking.)	*Traditional Native American, Traditional Mexican American, Traditional Female, and Low-income Urban Black* Global style. Holistic thinking is encouraged. Ways of knowing can include subjective and intuitive approaches. Artistic as well as intellectual pursuits are encouraged. Analytic areas such as math and science are discouraged for females.	Uses personalized and holistic approaches: Concepts presented in humanized story forms ("S" is a snake); analogies instead of dictionary definitions. May need to develop analytic style.
	Middle-class White Male Analytic style. Encouraged from young age to think abstractly. Emotions should not enter into thinking; thought should be logical, empirical.	Learns well from graphs, charts, formulas. May need to develop holistic approach to conceptual style.

Ramirez, Herold, and Casteneda (1975) argue that one's cognitive style, in the broadest sense, relates to more than modes of conceptualizing; it relates to differences in human relations, communication, and motivation which influence one's learning style. Two broad cognitive styles have been identified: "field independence" and "field dependence" (Ramirez *et al.* prefer the term "field sensitive" to "field dependence"). They have summarized research findings on these styles which are significant for educators as follows:

Field Sensitive (Field Dependent)	Field Independent
Perceives effect of the whole	Analyzes parts of the whole or re-arranges parts to make a whole
Concerned with social environment	Task centered
Sensitive to support or doubt from others	More independent of external judgment
Personal client-therapist relationship preferred	Formal client-therapist relationship preferred
Works cooperatively with others; likes to assist	Prefers to work independently and for individual recognition
Verbal proficiency	Skilled in spatial areas such as math and science concepts

Analysis of research on cultural patterns and learning styles in the areas of human relations, communication, and modes of conceptualizing, as the chart indicates, shows that oppressed groups in this country (women and Third World people) tend to be more field sensitive, whereas white males tend to be more field independent. It is the opinion of the author that school policies and practices and curriculum tend to be structured for field independence.

Implications for Self-Directed Learning

How should schools which emphasize self-directed learning relate to cultural differences in learning styles? Schools have aimed at producing at least a small group of students who have the qualities to be leaders and assume upper level responsibilities and status in society—young adults who can "cut the mustard" in a competitive situation. These may be aggressive individuals who can pursue goals independently or young people who can suppress their emotional concerns of humaneness and sensitivity to their own feelings and the feelings of others in order to allow the analytic and abstract part of the brain to proceed uninterrupted. This rugged individualism has been highly valued in terms of our behavior as a society;

honesty, liberty, and justice are valued only verbally. A highly intelligent and well informed person at the top of a law school class, an able speaker, such as Richard Nixon, could rise to the top office in the country with no demonstrated capacity for honesty. Our values for rugged individualism and analytic, rational thought are based primarily on a western European tradition.

Those who succeed best with these values are those of a northern European background, specifically males. Women are socialized into accepting a set of values associated with responsible behavior, friendliness, cooperativeness, and acceptance of authority. Girls who reject this feminine role, who are competitive, independent, and dominant, score higher on intelligence tests than girls who conform to that role (Kagan and Freeman, 1963; Sontag, Baker, and Nelson, 1958).

Those of a nonwestern cultural background, such as Mexican Americans, blacks, and Native Americans, tend to have a value orientation based on communal values and holistic thought processes. This is cultural rather than genetic. Some individuals have weaker racial/ethnic group identity due to factors such as being third generation into the country or interactive with the dominant culture, physically less identifiable as a member of the group, middle income, and/or not associated with a religious group having a strong racial/ethnic cultural component. These individuals can easily choose to give up or modify racial/ethnic minority cultural values and associated behaviors. In fact, middle-class cultural identity has been necessary to gain the economic resources of the society such as a good job, education, and a house in a middle class neighborhood.

Should we design self-directed learning environments to foster learning styles and characteristics of independence, aggressiveness, and analytic thought which are rewarded in the dominant society? Should women and racial/ethnic minorities consider their cultural heritage of field sensitivity in terms of cognitive style and interpersonal relationships a barrier to achievement and self-directed learning? If not, how can women and racial/ethnic minorities gain access to society's rewards? We need to consider the costs to individuals and to society of following this path. The white middle-class male who follows his cultural tradition, while gaining power, status, and financial rewards, has suffered. Heart attacks, stomach ulcers, and the earlier death rate of men compared to women, Rosenfeld argues, can be partially explained by the cultural pressure on men to succeed and gain prestige and status (Rosenfeld, 1972). Gail Sheehy (1976) also documents the problems of the male in his 40's, that is, successful career men who are suffering in terms of human relationships.

Sandra Bem (1975), a social scientist who has researched sex roles, comments on adjustment and achievement in relation to sex roles:

High masculinity in males has been related to better psychological adjustment during adolescence, but it is often accompanied during adulthood by high anxiety, high neuroticism, and low self-acceptance. Boys who are strongly masculine and girls who are strongly feminine tend to have lower overall intelligence, lower spatial ability, lower creativity.

In addition, it seems that traditional sex typing necessarily restricts behavior. Because people learn, during their formative years, to suppress any behavior that might be considered undesirable or inappropriate for their sex, men are afraid to do "women's work" and women are afraid to enter "man's world." Men are reluctant to be gentle, and women to be assertive. In contrast, androgynous people are not limited by labels. They are able to do what they want, both in their behavior and feelings.

Ramirez, Herold, and Casteneda (1975) argue that a Mexican American who is bicognitive, able to function in both a field independent and field sensitive manner, will be most able to function both within his/her own ethnic group and in the dominant society. Vernon Dixon (1971) speaks of the value of the "diunital" approach of many blacks in this country. It would seem, then, that the goals of a school designed for self-responsible behavior should allow both males and females, and both racial/ethnic minority and majority students to develop flexibility in terms of conceptual style and interpersonal relationships. Schools would need to be skilled in diagnosing students' learning styles, and in designing an environment which is conducive to different learning styles. Although there are culturally different learning styles, there is individual variation among racial/ethnic and sex groups. Teachers may be aware that cultural patterns exist, but it is essential that they develop skills to observe a student in order to determine his/her individual learning style.

All children would be more comfortable in a learning environment which is predominantly matched with their individual learning style in the earlier grades. As students progress and confidence is built, they can learn to be bicultural by experiencing learning environments which are not matched with their style. This should be true for white as well as racial/ethnic minority students, and male as well as female students. The goal should not, however, be solely transition for the racial/ethnic minority student to the learning style of the dominant group in society.

Hopefully, this flexibility would not create conformity—a new amalgamation of males, females, racial/ethnic majorities and minorities, so that one person was indistinguishable from another. Rather, one would hope both racial/ethnic minorities and whites, both males and females, would retain their own self-directedness to make choices and be flexible in a cultural environment with diverse values and behaviors.

Only by taking a bicultural approach can racial/ethnic minority students develop the ability to cope in the larger society, as well as maintain relationships and their ability to function within their own group. Only by taking this approach can women assume significant and diversified roles in society while maintaining flexibility to experience the range of human characteristics. Only by taking this approach can men, in particular white men, regain their full humanity, capacity for emotional expressiveness, and, perhaps, another ten years of life.

Will society accept such flexible, fully developed, competent, and caring persons?

Forces Which Affect Self-Direction
and Self-Responsibility
of Students

Alberto M. Ochoa and Ana Maria Rodriguez

Students' self-direction and self-responsibility are conditioned by what is expected from them by the teacher and the school system. Traditionally, schools have socialized students according to our society's values. In school students learn how they must think, believe, feel, and behave to be competent members of the society. Schools train, assort, and accredit the individual in a manner which fits our particular economic system. Those students whose values, language, and culture differ from those of the school curricula have the choice of either assimilating into the values of the dominant culture or being identified as linguistically and culturally deficient by the education system (Kjolseth, 1973; Cornoy, 1974; Bowles and Gintis, 1976).

Socioeconomic Forces

The history of our economy is closely linked with our educational history. Mass education came into being because workers were needed to maintain production lines. In the 19th century, education began serving the economy by providing workers who knew their place, were productive, and who also were subservient. Education produced workers with values that included dependability, the ability to follow directions and rules, and loyalty with little or no questioning of authority figures (Bowles and Gintis, 1976; Katz, 1971; Heilbroner, 1960).

At the turn of the century, the family was no longer adequate in providing training as the skills required for jobs were changing so rapidly. The rise of progressive education between 1890 and 1930 in the United States stressed education as the great equalizer. However, curricular and ability tracking, educational testing, the emphasis upon following directions, and the ultimate authority of administrators and teachers made education a system for integrating new workers into the labor force. It became evident in the 30's that the amount of education attained by an individual in the U.S. was dependent on one's race and economic level (Bowles and Gintis, 1976; Bell, 1973; Gintis, 1971; Blau and Duncan, 1967; Jencks *et al.*, 1972).

Today, the major role of schools can still be viewed as a way to produce a labor force for our economy. Education in the 1970's can be equated with the production of good workers having certain personality characteristics desired by the employer such as respect for authority, response to external incentives, and dependability. Through a grading system, schools reward these traits and discourage others. This means that schools are shaping the self-concepts, aspirations, and social class identification of our youth to fit the requirements of the social division of labor (Robertson, 1973; Reich, 1972; Bowles and Gintis, 1976).

The educational management practices of our schools reinforce social class identification and inequality through the application of theories that guide production in our industries. Theories such as Argyris' (1971) "Immaturity-Maturity," Herzberg's (1959) "Management Systems," Hersey and Blanchard's (1969) "Leader Effectiveness Model," McClelland's (1953) "Achievement Motivation," Skinner's (1953) "Behavior Modification-Reinforcement Theory," and Maslow's (1954) "Hierarchy of Needs" are part of our educational approaches in diagnosing the maturity (self-direction and self-responsibility) of the student for the purpose of molding him/her to the values, behaviors, and expectations of our economic system.

Cultural Forces

Because our schools traditionally have been oriented toward conformity, cultural diversity has been grossly ignored. Unfortunately, the educational system in the U.S. has failed to take into account the culturally unique set of learning, communication, behavioral, and relational styles that culturally and linguistically distinct students bring with them to the school as their normal learning tools (Steward and Steward, 1973; Ten Houten, 1971; Ramirez and Price-Williams, 1974; DeAvila and Havassy, 1974; Witkin, 1967; Cohen, 1969).

More recently, with the advent of legislation for mandatory equal educational opportunity (Lau, 1974) educators have been forced to integrate the student's cultural experience into the learning environment. However, translating the notion of cultural diversity into the program of instruction has proven a challenge for schools. Most of the literature which addresses the concept of pluralistic education reveals a limited interpretation of culture. To be specific, many educators seem to infer that recognition of students' cultures implies bringing to light only the historical contributions and deeds of people from various ethnic groups. Along with the historical perspective, other interpretations of culture include the representation of cultural traditions such as holidays, costumes, music, dance; and cultural art forms such as weaving, pottery, and jewelry making. Hence, instructional programs and curricula are designed to expose students to these kinds of cultural productions.

As a direct result of this type of emphasis on explicit culture, ethnically different students across the country are learning traditional dances, tasting ethnic foods, and reading about historical accomplishments which heretofore have been overlooked in the texts.

In line with this trend, the teachers of these ethnic students are specializing in university training programs which are said to introduce them to theories and methods of operationalizing the above described interpretations of culture into classroom programs. The reality is that bilingual teachers are offered courses in ethnic studies which are primarily history oriented, and methods courses which for the most part reinforce concepts of culture as objects and events.

There is no evidence to support educators' attempts to foster pluralistic attitudes through a presentation of history and cultural traditions alone. However, teachers and teachers of teachers continue to present explicit cultural variables as though they were the essence of cultural experience; and as though examination of these will lead to more pluralistic attitudes.

On the contrary, such a superficial interpretation of culture leads to the creation of neo-stereotypes. For example, the stereotypic image of Mexicans eating hot, spicy foods is as false as the notion that all Americans eat hamburgers. Similarly, to portray the Hispanic culture as typified by maracas, sombreros, or the Mexican Hat Dance is equally misguided. Nevertheless, instructional activities which are purportedly designed to give recognition to the culture of ethnic group students invariably hinge on just such objects and symbols of a culture. Granted, these items may have a place in one's cultural repertoire. But they are hardly the stuff by which cultural experience is formed, especially when taken out of a life's context.

A contrasting appraisal of what is needed to effect culturally pluralistic education has been offered by anthropologists, sociologists, and linguists alike. Authors in these disciplines have suggested that viable pluralistic education requires teacher cognizance of implicit cultural variables such as styles of communication, learning, and behavior (Hall, 1969; Lesser et al., 1965; Ramirez et al., 1975; Scheflen, 1974). Unlike foods, costumes, and artifacts, these factors of culture are not visible or tangible; they cannot be brought into the classroom for examination and display. Yet it is the cultural differences occurring at these subconscious levels which contribute to human conflict both in and outside of the classroom (Philips, 1972; Byers and Byers, 1972; Ramirez *et al.*, 1975).

The following are some examples of the kinds of dysfunctions which researchers have reported as evidenced between teachers and students of different cultural orientations.

Byers and Byers (1972) have cited the unhappy case study of the white teacher and black child who keep missing each other's cues in attempting to establish contact with one another. When the child looks to the teacher for nurturance or support, the teacher is not responsive. Conversely, the child does not look up at the teacher when the child is being signaled for individual help or attention. The observable result is that they never achieve the eye or body contact both are seeking. Because of unperceived cultural differences in their respective communication systems which prescribe different behaviors, teacher and student never seem to be able to attain a mode of interaction which is rewarding and satisfying to both.

Dysfunction occurs because cultural differences exist between the cultural systems of the students and their teachers. It is precisely this type of cultural difference which affects cross-cultural interaction both in and out of the classroom. The observable consequences of cross-cultural communication failures are varied and in most instances quite serious. For the classroom-aged child, these clashes with teachers undoubtedly mean rejection, frustration, and failure.

Moreover, studies have shown that well-meaning "mainstream" teachers who are not aware of the contrasting behavioral and perceptual patterns of their ethnic students tend to impose their own cultural rules for communicating, learning, and behaving upon these students. Teachers go even further in demanding that students perform competently in cognitive modes and social structures which are, perhaps, not toally familiar to them (Ramirez *et al.*, 1975; Philips, 1972). Again, the obvious outcome for children placed in unaccustomed classroom environments in which they are continually evaluated is failure. They are frequently labeled "slow learners," "M.R.," "disadvantaged," or "learning disabled." They are then channeled into the bottom group of the school's academic tracking system where they may be relegated for the remainder of their school lives (Stent *et al.*, 1973).

Sociopsychological Forces

Aragon's (1973) research on the self-concept and psychological development examines a process of psychological adjustment that affects all linguistically and culturally distinct students through their school years. According to Aragon, the acculturation syndrome is a process of five stages that the child goes through in order to maintain the culture of his/her home while developing the coping skills to participate in the dominant culture. The school, at the same time, sees the student as needing adjustment to the school climate and also lacking in motivation, incentive, and the need to achieve.

The violence of the acculturation syndrome begins in any school setting of any minority community in the U.S. where the teaching staff is culturally deficient in attempting to teach culturally distinct children. The child, instead of finding support and enrichment of the culture he/she brings to school, is slowly assimilated into the dominant monoculture of the school. The student's culture, language, and economic background play no role in the school curriculum.

The educational response that for the most part assimilates children into the dominant culture consists of four stages, with few reaching a fifth stage of "biculturalism" (Aragon, 1973, pp. 1-27; Murrillo, 1976, pp. 15-25):

Stage I is acceptance. The child has received a very strong influence from the home, both culturally and linguistically, and has learned love and security in the home environment. Before the age of six, the child has been told by the family that he/she will be starting school soon and thus is being mentally prepared. The child by now holds a strong sense of confidence in the parents' advice. However, soon the parents will betray the child when he/she is registered in school. The child senses this betrayal during the first few days of school.

Stage II is bewilderment. The institution the parents have told the child was good for him/her has begun the process of confusion. The child is told not to speak Spanish in or out of the classroom, and senses that this language is not the right language to be spoken. The teacher may proceed to tell the child that his/her diet is also inferior, upon presenting to the class the government-approved dietetic charts. The child becomes bewildered as a result of being confronted with different values and interpretation. The cultural values learned at home are in direct conflict with those that ensure success at school.

Stage III is rejection. The child is aware that the values learned at home are obstacles to success and are also sources of embarrassment. A love-hate process begins. The child begins to hate all the obstacles to school success: customs, language, diet, clothes, social patterns. The child's whole culture makes him/her different; at the same time, the child feels a strong love for his/her family and their language, customs, and social patterns. It is in these that the child feels secure, loved, and accomplished.

Stage IV is pseudo-acculturation. The child who reaches this stage, by now, has undergone profound psychological harrassment. It is at this stage that the child goes through cultural indecision and is continually confused as to what cultural behaviors he/she prefers. If the pressure is great by the dominant society, the child will assimilate its cultural behaviors.

Stage V is biculturate. If the child is able to survive stage IV and the dominant culture's social pressures, he/she reaches the stage of the psychological syndrome where able to participate in both cultures, that of the dominant society and his/her own.

Through the acculturation syndrome, the school system pressures ethnic minority students to assimilate the values of the dominant society while eliminating the use of their home language and culture.

Socioeducational Forces

The authors view the goals of the educational system and economic system as one and the same—increased productivity. Performance on the job is rewarded by money, status, and recognition. Performance in the school is rewarded by grades, status, and recognition. Those who produce according to the criteria of our schooling and economy are chosen to fill positions with decision-making influence (Reich, 1972; Bowles and Gintis, 1976; Illich, 1970).

The domesticating power of our schools in molding individuals who are unable to be critical of their learning and growth is evident in the following conditions (Freire, 1971, p. 59):

a. The teacher teaches and the students are taught;

b. The teacher knows everything and the students know nothing;

c. The teacher thinks and the students are thought about;

d. The teacher acts and the students have the illusion of acting through the action of the teacher;

e. The teacher chooses the program content and the students (who are not consulted) adapt to it.

It is, of course, possible for people to learn this way. Much of what you and I acquired in school was deposited by teachers. Most educational relationships outside of school take the same form; we use books, films, television, art, and people as veins of information that can be mined for our improvement. What we learn is often useful for our survival, and for our development.

But too many of the educational relationships we experience condition us to be consumers rather than producers of knowledge and ideas. They teach us how to adjust to the world rather than shape it to our needs and dreams. We end up well-educated about the world as it is, but often without the capacity to project better solutions for old problems or to grapple with new problems that face us. Most of us learn not to see ourselves as active agents, and we end up losing our capacity to learn what is needed to be active. Educational alienation may be as common in universities as in kindergartens or adult education programs; volume of knowledge or years of study is no guarantee that one has learned how to be an active subject in his/her own history. The ability to be self-responsible for one's learning, career goals, and problem solving is directly related to the nature of the learning environment created by teachers.

Instead of awareness of ourselves we are made aware of the values of others. Instead of possible models for a better society, we are usually taught a series of myths that bind us to the way things are. We too often learn to compete rather than to cooperate, to believe our needs will be met best by individual rather than collective action. Instead of being led to realize our tremendous potential, we usually are overwhelmed by how little we know. Instead of learning to learn, many of us are trained to look up to the experts with the answers. In almost all cases "education is defined as the transmission of beliefs," ideas, or information from one who knows to one who should know (Freire, 1971; Illich, 1971). Freire (1971) calls this "banker education": the dominant concept is that there exists a wealth of knowledge which can be deposited in the head of the learner, there to generate some interest, perhaps.

Classroom Alternatives

As indicated by the foregoing discussion, our economic system has largely influenced mass education. In turn, education for conformity by definition excluded ethnic minority children. Through the years this exclusion has taken any number of forms. It has manifested itself in the form of racial and linguistic isolation. It has been cited by Rosenthal as the lack of teacher expectation to perform. Earlier in this section, we discussed the exclusion which occurs as a result of student/teacher cultural dissonance. For the ethnically different student, schools have always been isolating.

Many educational alternatives have been suggested which address student exclusion and allow ethnically different students the opportunity to work and develop as independent, responsible learners. Ramirez and Casteneda (1974) have advocated educating toward bicognitive learners. Their premise is that ethnically different students must be prepared to function in mainstream settings and in their community settings as well. Hence, the authors recommend that students be taught in two modes or cognitive styles, field sensitive and field independent, until they become versed equally in both.

As a result of her study in the Warm Springs Indian community, Philips (1972) has suggested to educators that the participant structures familiar to students in their home communities should be adopted by the school. She contends that Warm Springs Indian students were not achieving in the classroom because the rules for participating in the classroom differed from those in effect in the reservation. According to Philips, students were either not prepared to participate in an unknown social system or they simply refused to participate in a system they considered belonged to an outsider.

Paulo Freire offers educators an alternative to the "banking system of education" (1973, pp. 136-64). He suggests four principles for promoting self-responsibility and self-direction in the educational process of our students:

1. All education requires some thought about people and society. Failure to think about people could lead to educational programs designed to dominate and subjugate. Failure to think about society produces an educational effort that is irrelevant.

2. The capacity of people to affect society, to change it, to make it more appropriate to their needs, results from reflection on themselves. Education should make people more aware of their world and their relationship to it.

3. What people are depends on their relationships to other beings, and to things. The more people are related to others, the more fully they are developed. Education should make people more aware of their world and their relationship to it.

4. The world people live in is in large measure created by themselves. People construct their social and cultural environment by building and breaking relationships; by creating and recreating the shape of their own history. To the extent that they act and their actions are the product of their reflections on themselves and their world, then they are the subject of their own history. To the extent that they act unaware, or are inactive, they are objects. Education, then should increase the awareness people have of themselves, of their relationships with each other, and of their role as the creators of their own present and future.

Cazden (1972) advocates three methods for bridging cultural dissonance in the classroom. Her first approach with black and Chicano students was to become familiar with the students by walking each child home and by inviting children to visit her home and community. Second, Cazden suggests building a shared life of memorable classroom experiences. Memorable events in her classroom included visits from friends, teachers, and parents, many of which were documented with pictures and audiotapes used in future sharing and reminiscing. A third way to lessen distance is to avoid classroom activities that may tend to increase it such as the salute to the flag. While some teachers may take exception to this last suggestion, saluting can be justified only if teachers are willing to make the activity more relevant to ethnically and linguistically different students.

Conclusion

Although the means which have been suggested here are varied, the end goal of these educational alternatives is the same. It is to make education more responsive to the culturally influenced learning differences among students. Schools and more specifically teachers must consider the cognitive and affective aspects of how children learn. Only when the appropriate teaching styles and learning environments are provided will the culturally distinct student be allowed to enjoy the learning experience, achieve, and develop as a self-responsible, self-initiating learner.

References

Juan Aragon. *Cultural Conflict in the Traditional Curriculum.* Sacramento: California State Department of Education, 1973.

Kenneth Addison. "A Theoretical Framework for a Psychologically-Oriented Curriculum for Low-Income Urban Black Youth." Unpublished doctoral dissertation. Madison: University of Wisconsin, 1976.

Tomas A. Arciniega. *Problems and Issues in Preparing Teachers of Bicultural Chicano Youngsters.* San Diego: Institute for Cultural Pluralism, San Diego State University, 1976.

Chris Argyris. *Management and Organization Development: The Path From AX to YB.* New York: McGraw-Hill Book Company, 1971.

J. Baratz. "Linguistic and Cultural Factors in Teaching English to Ghetto Children." *Elementary English* 46:199-203; 1969.

Diana Baumrind. "From Each According to Her Ability." *School Review*, February 1972, pp. 161-97.

Daniel Bell. *The Coming of Post-Industrial Society.* New York: Basic Books, 1973.

Sandra L. Bem. "Androgeny vs. the Tight, Little Lives of Fluffy Women and Chesty Men." *Psychology Today*, September 1975, pp. 56-62.

Andrew Billingsley. *Black Families in White America.* Englewood Cliffs, New Jersey: Prentice-Hall, Inc., 1969.

Peter Blau and Otis D. Duncan. *The American Occupational Structure.* New York: John Wiley & Sons, 1967.

S. Boggs. "The Meaning of Questions and Narratives to Hawaiian Children." In: Cazden *et al., op. cit.*

Samuel Bowles and Herbert Gintis. *Schooling in Capitalist America.* New York: Basic Books, Inc., 1976.

Annemarie Brewer. "On Indian Education." Unpublished paper, n.d.

P. Byers and H. Byers. "Nonverbal Communication and the Education of Children." In: Cazden *et al., op. cit.*

A. Casteneda and M. Ramirez. *Cultural Democracy, Bicognitive Development, and Education.* New York: Academic Press, 1974.

Courtney B. Cazden *et al.*, editors. *Functions of Language in the Classroom.* New York: Teachers College Press, 1972.

Cedric Clark. "The Concept of Legitimacy in Black Psychology." In: Edgar C. Epps, editor. *Race Relations.* Cambridge, Massachusetts: Winthrop Publishers, Inc., 1973. pp. 332-54.

R. Cohen. "Conceptual Style, Culture Conflict, and Nonverbal Tests of Intelligence." *American Anthropologist* 71:840-61; 1969.

Martin Cornoy. *Education as Cultural Imperialism.* New York: David McKay Company, Inc., 1974.

Virginia Crandall *et al.* "Parents' Attitudes and Behaviors and Grade School Children's Academic Achievement." *Journal of Genetic Psychology* 104:53-66; 1964.

Kent J. Davis and Herbert J. Klausmeier. "Cognitive Style and Concept Identification as a Function of Complexity and Training Procedures." *Journal of Educational Psychology* 61:423-30; December 1970.

E. A. DeAvila and B. I. Havassy. *I.Q. Tests and Minority Children.* Austin: Dissemination Center for Bilingual/Bicultural Education, 1974.

Vernon J. Dixon. "Two Approaches to Black-White Relations." In: Vernon J. Dixon and Badi G. Foster, editors. *Beyond Black or White: An Alternate America.* Boston: Little, Brown and Co., 1971.

R. V. Dumont. "Learning English and How to be Silent: Studies in Sioux and Cherokee Classrooms." In: Cazden *et al., op. cit.*

Jack D. Forbes. "Teaching Native American Values and Cultures." In: James A. Banks, editor. *Teaching Ethnic Studies.* Washington, D.C.: National Council for the Social Studies, 1973.

Badi G. Foster. "Toward a Definition of Black Referents." In: Vernon J. Dixon and Badi G. Foster, editors. *Beyond Black or White: An Alternate America.* Boston: Little, Brown and Co., 1971.

Paulo Freire. *Education for Critical Consciousness.* New York: The Seabury Press, 1973.

Paulo Freire. *Pedagogy of the Oppressed.* New York: Herder and Herder, 1971.

Herbert Gintis. "Education, Technology, and the Characteristics of Worker Productivity." *American Economic Review,* May 1971.

J. David Greenstone and Paul E. Peterson. *Race and Authority in Urban Politics.* New York: Russell Sage Foundation, 1973.

Edward T. Hall. *The Hidden Dimension.* New York: Doubleday/Anchor, 1969.

Paul Hersey and Kenneth H. Blanchard. *Management of Organizational Behavior.* Englewood Cliffs, New Jersey: Prentice-Hall, Inc., 1969.

Robert L. Heilbroner. *The Worldly Philosophers.* New York: Simon & Schuster, 1960.

Frederick Herzberg, B. Mausner, and Barbara Snyderman. *The Motivation to Work.* Second edition. New York: John Wiley & Sons, Inc., 1959.

Joseph E. Hill. "The Educational Sciences." Bloomfield Hills, Michigan: Oakland Community College, Institute for Educational Sciences, 1974.

V. Horner and J. Gussow. "John and Mary: A Pilot Study in Linguistic Ecology." In: Courtney Cazden and John Hymes, editors. *Functions of Language in the Classroom.* New York: Teachers College Press, 1972.

Judith Jaynes Hunsaker. *Sex Role Expectations in Parents of Recently Born Children.* Unpublished doctoral dissertation. Milwaukee: University of Wisconsin-Milwaukee, 1978.

Ivan Illich. *Deschooling Society.* New York: Harper & Row, Publishers, 1971.

I. L. Janis and P. B. Field. "Sex Differences and Personality Factors Related to Persuadability." In: I. L. Janis *et al.,* editors. *Personality and Persuadability.* New Haven, Connecticut: Yale University Press, 1959.

Christopher Jencks *et al. Inequality: Reassessment of the Effect of Family and Schooling in America.* New York: Basic Books, 1972.

V. P. John. "Styles of Learning—Styles of Teaching: Reflections on the Education of Navajo Children." In: Cazden *et al., op. cit.*

Mrs. Lyndon B. Johnson. "Introduction." Head Start Summer Program Brochure, 1965; reprinted in: Annie Stein. "Strategies for Failure." *Harvard Educational Review* 41(2):157; May 1977.

J. Kagan and M. Freeman. "Relation of Childhood Intelligence, Maternal Behaviors, and Social Class to Behavior During Adolescence." *Child Development* 34:899-911; 1963.

J. Kagan and H. A. Moss. *Birth to Maturity: A Study in Psychological Development.* New York: John Wiley & Sons, 1962.

Michael Katz, editor. *School Reform: Past and Present.* Boston: Little, Brown and Company, 1971.

R. Kjolseth. "Bilingual Education Programs in the United States: For Assimilation or Pluralism?" In: P. R. Turner, editor. *Bilingualism in the Southwest.* Tucson: University of Arizona Press, 1973.

Louis L. Knowles and Kenneth Prewitt. *Institutional Racism in America.* Englewood Cliffs, New Jersey: Prentice-Hall, Inc., 1969.

W. Labov. "Some Sources of Reading Problems of Negro Speakers of Non-Standard English." In: J. Baratz and R. Shuy, editors. *Teaching Black Children to Read.* Washington, D.C.:Center for Applied Linguistics, 1969.

W. Labov, P. Cohen, C. Robbins, and J. Lewis. "A Study of the Non-Standard English of Negro and Puerto Rican Speakers in New York City." Cooperative Research Project #3288. New York: Columbia University Press, 1968. pp. 339-48.

Lau v. *Nichols*, United States Supreme Court, 414 U.S. 563 (1974).

G. Lesser, D. Fifer, and D. Clark. "Mental Abilities of Children from Different Social Class and Cultural Groups." *Monographs of the Society for Research and Child Development*, 1965.

Rensis Likert. *New Patterns of Management.* New York: McGraw-Hill Book Company, 1961.

Eleanor Maccoby and Carol Nagy Jacklin. "What We Know and Don't Know About Sex Differences." *Psychology Today*, December 1974, pp. 109-12.

Martin L. Maehr and Pamela C. Rubovits. "Teacher Expectations: A Special Problem for Black Children with White Teachers?" In: Martin L. Maehr and William M. Stallings, editors. *Culture, Child and School.* Monterey, California: Brooks/Cole Publishing Co., 1975.

Abraham H. Maslow. *Motivation and Personality.* New York: Harper and Row, Publishers, 1954.

David C. McClelland *et al. The Achievement Motive.* New York: Appleton-Century-Crofts, 1953.

Minorities and Education. New York: Foundation for Change, 1973.

Harry Morgan. "Towards a Theory of Selected Knowledge Acquisition Patterns Among Black Children." Paper presented at the Annual Meeting of American Association for the Advancement of Science, Denver, Colorado, February 25, 1977.

Nathan Murillo. "The Mexican American Family." In: Carol A. Hernandez *et al.*, editors. *Chicanos—Social and Psychological Perspectives.* St. Louis: The C. V. Mosby Company, 1976.

Julius Nyerere. *Ujamaa: Essays on Socialism.* London: Oxford University Press, 1968.

David R. Olson. "What is Worth Knowing?" *School Review* 82(1); November 1973.

F. W. Ohnmacht. "Effects of Field Independence and Dogmatism on Reversal and Nonreversal Shifts in Concept Formation." *Perceptual and Motor Skills* 22:491-97; 1966.

A. Harry Passow. "Instructional Content for Depressed Urban Centers: Problems and Approaches." In: A. Harry Passow *et al.*, editors. *Education for the Disadvantaged.* New York: Holt, Rinehart and Winston, 1967. p. 352.

Wilfred Pelletier. "For Every North American Indian That Begins to Disappear, I Also Begin to Disappear." Neewin Publishing Co., n.p., n.d.

S. U. Philips. "Participant Structures and Communicative Competence: Warm Springs Children in Community and Classroom." In: Cazden *et al., op. cit.*

Henry Ramirez. "Teachers and Students: Differences in Teacher Interaction With Mexican Americans and Anglo Students." Washington, D.C.: U.S. Commission on Civil Rights, n.d.

M. Ramirez and A. Casteneda. *Cultural Democracy, Bicognitive Development, and Education.* New York: Academic Press, 1974.

Manuel Ramirez, P. Leslie Herold, and Alfredo Casteneda. *New Approaches to Bilingual, Bicultural Education*. Austin: The Dissemination and Assessment Center for Bilingual, Bicultural Education, 1975.

Manuel Ramirez, III, and D. R. Price-Williams. "Cognitive Styles of Children of Three Ethnic Groups in the United States." *Journal of Cross-Cultural Psychology*, 1974.

Michael Reich. "The Evolution of the U.S. Labor Force." In: Richard Edwards *et al.*, editors. *The Capitalist System*. Englewood Cliffs, New Jersey: Prentice-Hall, Inc., 1972.

Ross M. Robertson. *History of the American Economy*. New York: Harcourt, Brace, Jovanovich, 1973.

Albert Rosenfeld. "Why Men Die Younger." Condensed from Star Sunday Magazine of the *Kansas City Star*. Reprinted in: *Reader's Digest*, November 1972.

R. Rosenthal and H. L. Jacobson. *Pygmalion in the Classroom*. New York: Holt, Rinehart and Winston, 1966.

Alfred Scheflen. *How Behavior Means*. New York: Doubleday & Co., 1974.

Lisa A. Serbin and K. Daniel O'Leary. "How Nursery Schools Teach Girls to Shut Up." *Psychology Today*, 1975, pp. 57-58, 102-103.

Gail Sheehy. *Passages*. New York: E. P. Dutton, 1976.

Barbara A. Sizemore. "Educational Research and Desegregation: Significance for the Black Community." *The Journal of Negro Education* 47(1):58-68; Winter 1978.

Barbara A. Sizemore. "Education for Liberation." *School Review* 81(3):389-404; May 1973.

B. F. Skinner. *Science and Human Behavior*. New York: The Macmillan Co., 1953.

Geneva Smitherman. *Talkin' and Testifyin'*. Boston: Houghton Mifflin Company, 1977.

I. W. Sontag, C. T. Baker, and V. L. Nelson. "Mental Growth and Personality Development: A Longitudinal Study." *Monograph of the Society for Research in Child Development* 23; 1958.

Annie Stein. "Strategies for Failure." *Harvard Educational Review* 41(2):161; May 1971.

Madelon D. Stent, William R. Hazard, and Harry N. Rivlin, editors. *Cultural Pluralism in Education*. New York: Appleton-Century-Crofts, 1973.

Margaret Steward and David Steward. "The Observation of Anglo, Mexican, and Chinese American Mothers Teaching Their Young Sons." *Child Development* 44(2):329-37; 1973.

Hilda Taba and Deborah Elkins. *Teaching Strategies for the Culturally Disadvantaged*. Chicago: Rand McNally and Co., 1966.

W. D. Ten Houten. *Cognitive Styles and the Social Order*. Final Report, Part II, O.E.O. Study Boo-5135, "Thought, Race and Opportunity," 1971.

Paul Torrance. Reported in: "Sexual Stereotypes Start Early." *Saturday Review*, October 15, 1971, p. 80.

Albert D. Ullman. *Sociocultural Foundations of Personality*. Boston: Houghton Mifflin Company, 1965.

E. I. Walker and R. Heyns. *An Anatomy for Conformity*. Englewood Cliffs, New Jersey: Prentice-Hall, Inc., 1962.

H. A. Witkin *et al*. *Personality Through Perception*. New York: Harper and Brothers, 1954.

H. A. Witkin. "A Cognitive-Style Approach to Cross-Cultural Research." *International Journal of Psychology*, 1967-2, pp. 233-50.

Carter G. Woodson. *The Miseducation of the Negro*. Washington, D.C.: Associated Press, 1933.

5.
Developing Self-Directed Learning Programs

Lois Jerry Blanchard

A Parable

Once there was a committee
comprised of good teachers.
They were bright, and concerned,
and educated, and well-meaning.
They wanted to help students
live in peace,
love each other,
be their brother's keeper,
love learning,
become self-directed.
Then someone said,
"We will teach by example."
Since they were
bright, and concerned,
and educated, and well-meaning,
they were sad.

Jon Rye Kinghorn (1978, p. 19)

What examples are taught by the human activities in school? Would these activities enhance self-directed learning? James B. Macdonald (1975) says that it is in the quality of living, in the activities of the school, that we will find the values of the school being taught and learned.

The Culture of the School—In Whose Interest?

What do children learn in school? Are they rewarded for creativity, for compliance? Are they encouraged to make decisions for themselves or to

This chapter was written by Lois Jerry Blanchard with contributions from Arthur L. Costa, Delmo Della-Dora, Mario Fantini, and Richard Foster.

accept direction without any question? Have they learned that some students are cherished more than others? Do they think this has to do with race or sex or economics? Do they act toward one another on the basis of this knowledge? Have they learned who the powerful are, about unchallenged authority, about being powerless? Are they learning to be free and responsible?

Those things which educators do in schools reflect their values. The kinds of behaviors that are rewarded, the ways in which students are categorized, the conditions of living with one another that are created, the student personality characteristics that are cherished, the attributes and skills that are prized by school personnel define the culture of the school. They constitute the institutional concept of "the good life."

The child readily learns what is valued and the system of norms which influence behavior in school. Obviously, children also learn from this whether or not they are valued as a person.

The truth of that statement is harsh, but consider the evident class structure in our schools. Students have names for it which change over the years: "frats," "jocks," "hooks," "greasers," "burnouts." Staff also have names for the class structure: "bluebirds," "college-bound," "potential dropout," "underachiever," "disruptive." This labeling is a part of the school culture, the system of beliefs, and consequent behaviors that make up the gestalt of a school.

Another aspect of the school culture that must be considered is the socialization process used to perpetuate societal values. An important function of socialization is to teach students what society expects of them and what it values. It is the means by which students are made ready for society.

In the first chapter of this publication, the author took the position that self-directed learning is representative of those characteristics of schooling which should distinguish education in a democratic society from that in autocratic societies. How does school make students ready for society? Through participatory decision making? Through bureaucratic hierarchies based on authoritarian control? Through contrived situations intended to provide a semblance of democracy in action? Through opportunities to choose what to learn, how to learn it, and how to evaluate progress?

"What contradictions do we see in the way schools presently operate that reflect discrepancies between our humane ideals and our political practices and that constitute a false consciousness? . . . How can we move from the question of 'who is messing up the schools' to the question of 'whose interests are being served by schooling'?" (Macdonald, 1975, p. 25).

If we are to seek an answer to the question, "In whose interest?", for our schools, we must consider the values people act on in school.

Values of the School and Self-Directed Learning

Values are reflected in the explicit goal statements of the school. They are also encompassed in the unstated goals of the school, the hidden curriculum. "The functions of the hidden curriculum have been variously identified as the inculcation of values, political socialization, training in obedience and docility, the perpetuation of traditional class structure—functions that may be characterized generally as social control" (Vallance, 1973-74). In reality, the hidden curriculum encompasses the values inherent in the school culture—people's beliefs about others, about education, about life—and the consequent behaviors.

What are the values that school teaches through behaviors toward others? Does it appear that people trust each other? Are children trusted to participate in planning their education? Are differences celebrated or rejected? How do methods reflect beliefs? Consider again the continuums (school-directed —→ mid-point —→ self-directed) described in Chapter 1 of this publication. In what direction is the school going? What values does that suggest it holds?

A comprehensive study of how a school's environment can and does impact on children was conducted in 1968 under the auspices of the National Institute of Mental Health. In describing the results of their study, the authors point out that the mode of authority children experience in schools affects the codes of behavior and the underlying values that children develop (Biber and Minuchin, 1970). The same authors predicted differences in the way youngsters from varying school environments "would think, perceive other people, emphasize and shape their concepts of themselves" (Minuchin, 1969). The findings of their study support this prediction and point out that: "The clearest and most consistent school related findings . . . were not in the area of cognitive functioning, but in the area of self-perception and attitude—matters of personal identity, perception of development and investment in roles" (Minuchin, 1969, p. 372).

Clearly this points out the impact of the unstudied or hidden curriculum and the need for school staff members to assess the value structure they are perpetuating through the conditions of living in the school environment they have created and implemented. Instrumentation for such an assessment and a comprehensive review of the hidden curriculum can be found in the study, *The Values of the School: A Study of Student and Staff Perceptions of the Goals of the School and the Hidden Curriculum"* (Blanchard, 1977). Your school goals are based on what *you* value. You will act accordingly and create a learning climate. Do your goals/values foster the concept of self-directed learning? The extent to which the school staff sees learners as participating in directing their own learning sets the limits for the extent to which students will make progress in this regard.

The Administrator and School Values

The administrator strongly influences the climate of the school—its culture, its concept of the good life, its values emphasis. If an administrator wishes to expand or initiate programs for self-directed learning, a first order of business would be to consider the culture of the school and its values emphasis. In doing this, the principal must necessarily assess his/her own values as well as the nature of interpersonal relationships, the extent of staff involvement in decision making, and the system of controls in use.

One way to start would be to assess one's own self-directedness. Look at the characteristics of the self-directed learner outlined in Chapter 1. The following examples from that section have been paraphrased. How do you see yourself? Do you

Have an attitude of wanting to take on increasing responsibility for your own learning (for your own growth)?

Regularly clarify your own values and establish educational goals that are consistent with these values?

Develop plans for achieving your goals?

Analyze the dynamics of the groups in which you participate and demonstrate capability of operating successfully in group decision-making processes?

Know when to ask for help or direction from others and are willing to ask for it as needed?

Prize human differences, including those related to race, sex, ethnicity, religious affiliation, and social class . . . use these differences to clarify and develop your own ideas and your own understandings of self and others?

Recognize that no one is ever truly alone for very long in learning processes because, ultimately, the quality of human interaction determines the quality and quantity of learning in a democratic society?

The Helping Professional

The administrator and teacher who would support self-directed learning for children and who themselves would be self-directed learners could be assumed to have the qualities of the helping professional as described by Arthur Combs in his important studies at the University of Florida. Behavior is an expression of beliefs (Combs *et al.*, 1969). Combs and his colleagues studied the belief systems of practitioners in some of the helping professions: teachers, counselors, professors, nurses, and Episcopalian priests. Successful, effective practitioners in these fields had certain beliefs in common. For example, they saw other people as

Able rather than unable
Friendly rather than unfriendly
Worthy rather than unworthy
Internally motivated rather than externally motivated
Dependable rather than undependable
Helpful rather than hindering (p. 33)

In addition these helping professionals saw themselves as:

Identified with, rather than apart from, others
Feeling adequate rather than inadequate
Feeling trustworthy rather than untrustworthy; as dependable, reliable, and having the potential to cope with events
Being wanted rather than unwanted; as likeable, capable of bringing forth a warm response in those important to him/her
Being worthy rather than unworthy; as a person of integrity, dignity, consequence, worthy of respect (p. 14)

Effective helping teachers bring these purposes to their work:

Freeing rather than controlling people. They see the helping task as one of assisting, releasing, facilitating rather than as controlling, manipulating, coercing, inhibiting behavior.
Being concerned with larger rather than smaller issues. They tend to view events in a broad rather than a narrow perspective.
Being self-revealing rather than self-concealing. They are willing to disclose the self . . . to be themselves.
Being personally involved with, rather than alienated from, the people they work with. The helper sees his/her appropriate role as one of commitment to the helping process and willingness to enter into interaction.
Being process-oriented rather than goal-oriented. They are concerned with furthering processes rather than achieving goals. They seem to see their appropriate role as one of encouraging and facilitating the process of search and discovery as opposed to promoting or working toward personal or preconceived goals (p. 15).

Also, helpers who are effective have a people rather than a things (objects, events, rules, regulations) orientation. They are likely to be more concerned with the perceptual experience of those they work with rather than the objective facts (p. 16).

"Human behavior is always purposeful. How the professional helper operates will be dependent upon what he believes are the purposes of those with whom he must work, the purpose of the particular kind of helping profession in which he is involved, and his own personal and professional purposes at any moment" (pp. 14-15).

Richard Copeland (1976) completed a study of administrative effectiveness in relation to the characteristics of the helping professional, including a useful assessment inventory. Another guide which may be used to assess readiness to initiate or support a program of self-directed learning has been developed by Delmo Della-Dora. Some items from this guide, *Elements of Self-Directed Learning: Self-Assessment of Interests and Abilities*, are included here. How would you code your interest and ability on these items? (Code: A = very high/excellent; B = high/good; C = fair/moderate; D = less than fair; E = poor/none.)

Interest   *Ability*

_____ 1. Helping students (staff) learn to clarify their own _____ values.

_____ 2. Helping students (staff) learn to clarify their _____ educational goals.

_____ 3. Helping students (staff) plan for achievement of _____ goals on an individual basis.

_____ 4. Helping students (staff) plan for achievement of _____ goals with others (particularly in small groups).

_____ 6. Helping students (staff) assess their own achieve- _____ ment and/or progress toward *individual* goals.

_____ 7. Helping students (staff) assess achievement of _____ and/or progress toward *group* goals.

_____ 10. Helping students (staff) learn how to operate _____ effectively in small group decision-making processes.

_____ 19. *Your* ability to provide administrative or super- _____ visory support and assistance to teachers who have an interest in becoming more skillful at self-directed approaches in teaching/learning.

_____ 20. Your ability to analyze and use information _____ about social-cultural forces at work in the classroom and the school for facilitation of instruction.

These questions become basic: Are you moving toward being a self-directed learner? Do you want to help others move in that direction? To what extent do you want to work with others to assess your group's readiness to develop programs which support self-directed learning? Are you interested in assessing your school's values and their support of self-directed learning activities?

Richard Foster has succinctly outlined the administrator's role in a letter he wrote as a member of the team working on this publication:

I believe the principal is a key figure in learning, self-directed or any learning. The functions of the principal include the following:
1. Creating an environment for instruction
2. Facilitating the instructional program
3. Selecting, assigning, reinforcing teachers
4. Evaluating the instructional program.
To carry this out, the principal must:
1. Be a teacher of teachers
2. Model self-directed learning in faculty meetings, planning sessions, interpersonal sessions, PTA meetings, etc.
3. Have high task skills in:
   a. Planning and problem solving
   b. Setting goals with staff and individual teachers
   c. Knowing an instructional program (that is, self-directed learning)
   d. Developing strategies of instructional movement
   e. Enjoying conflict management
   f. Growing and teaching from the critiquing process.
4. Have high human skills in:
   a. Communicating both verbally and nonverbally
   b. Encouraging people to solve their own problems
   c. Being a helping person—empathy, dignity, warmth, concreteness.

Staff Development Activities and Self-directed Learning

Having considered your own readiness, that of the staff, and the conduciveness of the school environment to initiate, expand, or support self-directed learning, what are some possible first steps?

Keep in mind that any staff development model chosen will have a philosophy inherent in it. The model may encourage participatory decision making; it may enhance self-directedness; it may be a lock-step, linear approach with prescribed activities; it may provide autocratic means to a democratic end. Again, consider the environment *it* creates.

There are many staff development plans. Find the one or adopt/adapt parts of several that make sense for you and those you work with each day. There is no one right way, as Mario Fantini indicates in his contribution to this section. He says:

. . . any administrator who wants to help teachers foster self-directed learning needs most of all to remember the words "options" and "choices." . . . Broadly speaking, *change is triggered in two basic ways: either people get pushed toward an idea or they are drawn toward it.* The history of educational change agents shows that both apparently may be effective depending upon the circumstances. The latter strategy, however, occasionally referred to as the "magnet strategy," maximizes direct individual and group participation since it allows individuals to make their own choices. The value of individual input is thereby stressed. In effect, an administrator offers up a number of ideas and then provides opportunities to identify with them.

You will notice that the staff development plans discussed here encourage individual and group participation. They are complementary and compatible with the positions on self-directed learning which have been expressed throughout this publication.

The "Whole Person" Approach to Inservice Education

Delmo Della-Dora describes an approach which he has successfully used many times to address a variety of inservice needs:

Inservice education has tended to focus either on specific new knowledge ("new" math, other new subject matter) and new skills (Flanders' interaction analysis, "discovery" teaching techniques) or on feelings and attitudes (values clarification techniques, self-concept enhancement activities). Still others, fewer in number, use simulation (role playing, psychodrama). Each approach has some merit, although approaches which focus primarily on new knowledge have traditionally shown the least promise of those noted.

Approaches which focus on all three dimensions of human behavior simultaneously seem to hold great promise. That is, educational processes which take into account knowledge/skills, feelings/attitudes, and overt behaviors will be recognizing that all these dimensions of humanness do interact simultaneously in every setting. In today's educational parlance, we must be aware of the cognitive, affective, and motoric (or psychomotoric) aspects of each person's being.

The Michigan-Ohio Regional Educational Laboratory (MOREL) developed an effective model for anti-racism inservice education of teachers based on this principle in 1968 and it has been used since in developing programs for self-directed learning. The MOREL model began with a self-assessment inventory which was completed by all teachers. The questions of the inventory asked participants to identify knowledge of the issues involved in racism, racist practices, and racial prejudice. They were also asked to indicate feelings or attitudes toward specific issues involved in schooling and race, and, finally, were asked to describe their own past behaviors/activities related to dealing with racial issues.

After analyzing the results, the MOREL staff provided new knowledge about the racial matters involved. Participants then indicated how they felt about the new information and what implications they saw for changing their own behavior as teachers.

Following this, a discussion was conducted concerning the alternative courses of action which might be pursued as a result of the new information and of the risks and consequences of each as perceived by individual teachers. These first phases emphasized knowledge (cognitive) and feelings (affective). Participants were encouraged to try out possible new behaviors that each thought might be desirable for them through role-playing the new behaviors in the group. Feelings about the tryout of the new behavior were then discussed. Following this, a support person or support group was identified to help each person as he/she decided when and how to try out the proposed new course of action in a real situation.

Participants reported their actions and any resultant new knowledge and feelings that accompanied them. This completed one cycle of new knowledge, with accompanying feelings and behavior. The MOREL staff then introduced new information based on apparent needs of the group, which initiated another "whole person" learning cycle. Ideally, the cycle is repeated until each participant is capable of initiating a new cycle based on understanding what would help him/her grow in the ability to be more effective as a teacher in any area of learning— whether it be to counter the effects of institutional racism or to develop approaches which will assist students in becoming more self-directed learners.

The "Beachhead" Approach

Richard Foster has found what he calls the "beachhead" approach to be effective in working with staff. When a need, such as for self-directed learning programs, has been identified, Foster proposes that the administrator work intensively with those people on his/her staff who are interested in the program. This group would establish its goals, develop plans, learn together, implement and evaluate their efforts. They would become a support group, offering help and encouragement to one another.

There are a number of benefits to such an approach. A smaller group can be more functional to work with especially on a large staff. There are different staff needs, styles, and varied readiness for acceptance of new ideas, differing attitudes toward change. Moving with those who are ready and giving the others an opportunity to wait and see is helpful. Those who are more hesitant to change may lose their reluctance once the program is underway, been observed as "do-able" and evaluated. Then, they, too, can become part of the project.

In a similar vein, Fantini states:

Attempts to create self-directed educational environments within school structures assume that organizational supports will be established. For example, it may be appropriate to call together teachers who are interested in the formation and implementation of self-directed learning approaches. Providing an organizational format to legitimize the work of the teachers who choose to join such groups is the responsibility of the administrator. It should be made clear to the teachers that they have the option to join the group or drop out of the group without penalty or stigma . . . the school administration cannot "push" any single self-directed option that all should choose. Rather, the structure should enable any teacher who so desires to participate in the project. Perhaps the self-directed plan developed can be a "subsystem" of the total school, serving as a type of R & D for the school as a whole, thus feeding important information back to the entire professional family.

The administrator provides organizational supports through being knowledgeable of the program, through sharing, through showing interest, through working as a planning team member.

The Team Planning Approach

Fantini discusses the concept of self-directed learning as well as the provision of organizational support through the team planning approach:

Given the fact of human diversity, it is sensible to plan various educational environments in order to match the varied learning styles of students with the way in which they are taught. One means to achieve this end which is held in esteem by many professional educators is the concept of self-directed learning.

Providing opportunities for students to control their own learning is based on the assumption that students should be able to choose from among a range of legitimate educational environments. It is difficult to conceive of *one* self-directed learning approach that could be purposefully imposed on all students, teachers, and parents. This is because some students may prefer to pursue other activities on their own, others in groups; some may have a preference to learn with teacher "A," others with teacher "B"; some may be attracted by the computer, others by peer tutors, others to action learning, and still others to multilanguage, multicultural contexts. Additionally, even among those who pursue self-directed learning approaches, some students, parents, and teachers may combine self-directed learning with self-study, others with a "programmed curriculum" in which students proceed through a series of carefully planned steps, and so on.

In short, no one pattern or combination of patterns is "better" than another for *all* students, only better for *some* students. Consequently, each legitimate self-directed pattern should have equal status with others. However, whatever the concept of self-directed learning, the common denominator is choice. . . .

Once groups of teachers emerge around different conceptions of self-directed learning, the administrator may want to continue facilitating further peer inter-action in order to promote the establishment of the organizational vehicle of team planning. At this stage, in keeping with our definition of self-directed learning as an alternative, it is of paramount importance to have much shared decision making. Without the support of teachers, administrators, and parents, most alternatives are in danger of having a very short life span. Before people can share in the decision-making process, they have to trust each other. Therefore, it is the responsibility of the administrator to ensure that self-directed learning is adequately discussed among interested parties prior to the formation of a planning group.

Once there is a general understanding of the meaning of self-directed learning, a team planning group can be made operational within the school organization. This team planning group might consider including community members in its efforts. The administrator must recognize that community members and teachers form the nucleus of participants in these groups. The role of the administrator is usually one of *facilitator*. Since these groups are made up of volunteers from the teaching staff and from the community, there is a good chance that previous interaction among group members will have been minimal. Therefore, the administrator who convenes the group must be knowledgeable with regard to the principles of group psychology. In particular, group members must be made to feel that they have an investment in the group's activities and they must be made aware of the consequences of their activities for themselves and for others.

Another important item in facilitating the efficient functioning of small groups is dealing with the tasks at hand based on a specific agenda—team planning groups are also task-oriented. It is often better to have a concrete item for discussion than a free flowing session which has no goal. Considering the important role of the teacher in encouraging self-directed learning, an overall strategy of organizational change as suggested by this paper needs to be underscored.

As facilitator, the administrator needs to be conscious of creating an atmosphere of openness in which people are encouraged to express their feelings. This can best be accomplished by the group leader's receptivity to the ideas of and support for each contributor. He or she should also pay special attention to extra verbal cues (facial expressions, posture). Usually, this mutually supportive attitude will spread through the group so that its members create a supportive environment for one another. The peer group interaction of teachers with teachers will help in the validation of the individual's feelings and also lend an air of credibility to how the group is perceived by those outside the group.

Team planning as a vehicle for designing self-directed learning environments must also be given organizational support in the form of providing time *during the school day* for teachers to do their planning. This time must be the same for all team members, although it need not be the same every day. The teachers can be from different grades and can be teaching different subjects. This planning team must not be perceived as merely an extra preparation period by either the teachers or the administration. Otherwise, it will become a dumping ground for all unwanted tasks. Usually, a group of instructional leaders together with the administrator will continue long-range planning efforts for the school with regard to self-directed learning.

Once fully operational, team planning can benefit from still another factor, the organizational support of an instructional leader, who will emerge from the ranks of the group itself. The various instructional leaders should also meet to choose a faculty coordinator who reports to faculty meetings and may create opportunities for dialogue about the schoolwide implications of self-directed learning. The faculty coordinator must also report regularly to the principal. Team planning also involves the evaluation of self-directed programs. When possible, this process should be ongoing throughout the school year and, at various junctures, should take student, parent, and teacher satisfaction into account.

Finally, an often influential organizational aspect that may advance self-directed alternatives concerns the reward system. It must be recognized that standardization of rewards reinforces established norms and encourages conformity; this may mediate against the diversity inherent in self-directed learning environments. Consequently, the rewards embraced under a self-directed learning philosophy should encourage pluralism in instructional approaches and a variety of ways of orchestrating resources within the school and community.

In sum, much has been learned over the past decade in our efforts with school reform. One set of lessons deals with the need to personalize learning and to offer a wider choice to the learners. Self-directed learning is an important advance in this direction.

The DDAE Approach

John Goodlad (1975) describes another approach to staff development, DDAE—dialogue, decisions, action, and evaluation. He points out that there are two fundamentally different views about how change occurs. One is rationalistic in bias: purpose precedes action. This gives rise to the assumption that schools "need only better and clearer goals and then their activities can be aligned with them. How good they are is then determined by evaluating the degree of goal achievement" (Goodlad, 1975, p. 112). The R, D, and D (research, development, and diffusion) model follows this form.

The other change theory that Goodlad cites takes the position that purpose, if any, follows or is discovered in action. Although Goodlad does not advocate either extreme, the staff development model he describes is "productive tension between an inner drive for renewal and ideas, services, and encouragement from without" (Goodlad, 1975, p. 113).

The process he discusses grew out of an array of relationships: teacher, administrator, staffs of other schools, community, Goodlad and his colleagues at the University of California/Los Angeles.

In time, teachers, principals, and members of our staff agreed on the need to improve the process of dialogue in schools and developed criteria for a process of DDAE—dialogue, decisions, action, and evaluation. Conducting business through such a process became a way of life for all of us. . . .

At the request of the schools, and to a degree on our own, we provided annotated bibliographies and readings on microfiche regarding current innovations and ideas for educational improvement. Clusters of teachers began to discuss possible new practices, to become curious about alternatives. A few, working together, began to try some things.

One of the most essential elements in what proved to be an exciting experience in inner-oriented change with support from the outside was the process of DDAE. In those schools developing high DDAE. . . . It appeared that many teachers were achieving increasing control over their own individual destinies and the conduct of daily life in the schools. . . .

The way in which specific changes or innovations emerged is interesting. There was very little fuss or fanfare. Possible educational changes entered rather naturally into the DDAE process. Teachers discussed and used them as they did textbooks, films, or any other resources. They simply tried what seemed to make sense, more or less "on the run," in the process of conducting and refining an educational program for children. The smoothness of execution, in many instances, would be somewhat dismaying or unnerving to those who think that all significant changes must be imposed systematically from without. . . .

The foregoing provides only a glimpse of what began with an attempted symbiosis of dissimilar organisms seeking to combine self-interest for mutual welfare, the synergy that resulted, and the serendipity we all came to appreciate. The League approach represents an alternative to R, D, and D as a strategy for school change and improvement. It does not rule out the usefulness of R, D, and D and its products, but these become meaningful after, not before, the people in a school begin to examine themselves and their settings through the process of DDAE. This approach does not rule out, either, the presence of interested, outside parties; in fact, they are essential. When those within the school begin to stir, they need to establish a relationship with sympathetic, constructively critical elements on the outside. Forces on the inside and forces on the outside establish a productive tension conducive to change. Perhaps the entire process is best left unnamed; but, if we must, "S, S, and S" will suffice—symbiosis, snyergy, and serendipity (Goodlad, 1975, pp. 115-16).

Goodlad sees purposes evolving from activity, from shared experiences: dialogue, discussion. Staff implements and evaluates activities and the sharing continues.

A Systems Approach

Some educators are more comfortable with a linear approach to program change. This systematic design became popular during the push for accountability. The steps in this staff development model are:

1. Needs assessment
2. Goals—broad statements of intent
3. Objectives—specific outcome statements intended to address goals
4. Delivery systems—activities designed to meet the objectives
   Delivery systems could include:
   a. methods
   b. materials
   c. organization
   d. staffing qualifications
   e. training needs—to implement delivery system
5. Evaluation—to assess that degree objectives have been met
6. Recommendations—for modification, dissemination, etc. (Waterford School District, 1976).

Critics of this kind of model contend that it is too lock-step and, consequently, does not encourage creative solutions. Proponents point out that the model can be entered at any step. For example, an especially effective classroom activity (delivery system) may give rise to the questions:
   a. Why did this work?
   b. Are there objectives that can be met better with this type of activity?
   c. What student needs are being addressed?
   d. What other materials could be used?

And thus, the purposes of the model are eventually addressed and, although they can then be reported out in linear fashion, that systematic approach has not dictated the actual development of the idea or program.

The Supervisory-Management Team Approach

In a recent NASSP publication, *How to Change Your School*, J. Lloyd Trump and William Georgiades (1978) suggest a Supervisory-Management Team. The leadership role is diffused through this approach.

It assumes that the principal will delegate important, but routine, responsibilities so that three-fourths or more of his/her time can be spent directly on the improvement of teaching and learning. The principal then establishes a team of staff members to assist in the curriculum change process.

Trump and Georgiades state that: "People are more likely to accept changes in schools when the persons in charge show willingness and effectiveness in following different patterns of leadership and supervision. The S-M team needs to understand the variety of values held among all the constituents of the organization. Resistance to change constitutes a major individual difference among persons. Therefore . . . a variety of programs with multiple options is essential in a school" (p. 57).

Trump and Georgiades also suggest some basic questions for consideration by the S-M team. Their publication reviews the use of sound teaching methods to be used in working with people to change schools. They caution:

> Schools also do not change because facilities, equipment, schedules, and other "things of education" change. Change is not brought about merely by building a new edifice, spending more money, buying new equipment, increasing supplies, and the like. Schools change only when the behaviors of persons who occupy schools change.
>
> Superficiality is an enemy of change. . . . It is easy to change schools simply by changing superficially the labels attached to different practices and not by actually altering the practices themselves. Thus the leadership role requires a complete understanding of the reasons for, the procedures involved, and the evaluation methodologies used in relation to all of the changes that are undertaken (pp. 52, 59).

Administrative and Supervisory Support Systems for Self-Directed Learning

Art Costa, Sacramento State University, contributed the following as another suggested approach to developing programs for self-directed learning.

> What can principals, supervisors, and other administrators do to help teachers who want to foster self-directed learning?
>
> I would open with the assumption that the administrator must create an atmosphere in which teachers experience certain conditions which promote self-directed learning. The administrator or supervisor who truly values self-directed learning would exhibit certain behaviors which model that value. Following are some of the behaviors which would be exhibited.
>
> *The administrator would value differences in teaching style.* Just as learners are different, so too, teachers are different. While most agree to this truism, the implementation of this principle is often neglected. Too often administrators or

supervisors tolerate differences in an attempt to convert colleagues and staff to their own way of thinking. Because teachers have variation in cognitive style, teaching style, and philosophical orientations, the administrator who values self-directed learning will facilitate having each teacher achieve his/her own goals using his/her own best means.

For example, within any one staff, there will undoubtedly be some teachers who feel that the major purpose of education is to develop students' intellectual powers, problem-solving abilities, and cognitive processes. These teachers might value such teaching strategies as inquiry, open-ended discussions, and other socratic techniques. Other teachers might view education as a way of transmitting certain values, concepts, and skills to students. These teachers may employ such teaching strategies as lecture, demonstration, and conceptual development techniques. Still other teachers may view the main purpose of education to be the development of each learner's inner potential, innate creativity, and emerging self-worth. These teachers may utilize teaching techniques including learning centers, class meetings, and emergent learning.

The administrator who values self-directed learning will value each of these philosophical positions on his/her staff. The question which must be asked is: Do all these teaching styles and philosophical orientations promote self-directedness in students? In other words, can the administrator who believes in, values, and strives for self-directedness in students have a repertoire of support behaviors which helps each teacher on the staff even though the administrator may view the teacher's style and orientation as counterproductive to the achievement of self-directedness in students?

If the administrator is viewed as an instructional leader, capable of supporting and facilitating the improvement of instruction, then the only answer to this dilemma can be that the administrator must model what he/she believes in. The behaviors which facilitate the self-directedness of teachers who in turn will facilitate the self-directedness of students will include the following:

1. *Facilitating the acquisition of accurate information.* Self-directedness implies making decisions for oneself. The adequacy of those decisions is based upon relevant data. The more substantial the data upon which the decision is based, the higher can be the quality of that decision. Therefore, the administrator will be able to gather or help others acquire such information about students, programs, test results, opinions of parents, feelings of staff, and reactions from trustees, so as to facilitate decision making by others.

2. *Refraining from making value judgments.* Self-directedness requires one to make judgments about his/her own actions, searching for the effects of actions in relation to the achievement of purposes. The administrator who makes value-judgments usurps the self-directedness of others. The teacher who depends upon others to make evaluations is not self-evaluative and, therefore, not self-directed. Knowing this, the wise administrator provides feedback, data, and information, then invites the teacher to make value inferences based on those data.

3. *Listening, accepting, and clarifying.* A climate of trust is built when administrators actively listen to, paraphrase, extend, build upon, clarify, and seek opinions from others. Teachers want to be listened to. Their ideas, experiments, questions, and problems should be explored, answered, and resolved by thinking them through themselves rather than having others supply results, alternatives, and solutions. Such dialogue is the necessary link between idea, theory, or hypothesis and action in practice. Modeling self-directedness by administrators means

providing a sounding board for others to think through their own strategies rather than making prescriptions for them.

4. *Structuring*. Administrators allocate certain resources of time, personnel, space, finances, and talent. Boards of trustees adopt policies which place constraints on these resources. In order for teachers to make best use of these resources, it is necessary for the administrators to spell out, identify, and communicate that structure under which the school and its personnel operate. Knowing these ground rules and constraints facilitates the teacher making the best decision about use of time, accomplishment of objectives, and consequences of decisions.

5. *Explicating a value system*. If teachers' values, philosophies, and styles are understood and accepted, the administrator then is in a position to communicate his/her own. This is not to mean that the administrator manipulates others into subscribing to his/her beliefs. Rather, as a member of the staff, he/she too is entitled to a philosophical value base. This should provide the administrator the opportunity to state, theorize about, and translate into practice his/her notions about self-directed learning. Knowing the administrator's value system and experiencing the positive effects of his/her modeling of that value system in dealing with others, maximizes the possibility that teachers will adopt, translate, and implement self-directed learning into their own classroom practices.

Change and Self-directed Learning

What can be learned from these approaches to change? That the leader is a key factor in change. That staff should have the option to be involved or not. That if they "opt in," they must have the opportunities to give direction to the change, to exercise participatory decision making. That those involved need on-going support systems and that they need environments and leaders that say: "You are worthy," "You can be trusted," "You are able." There need to be opportunities for knowing, valuing, and acting because participation in change is cognitive, affective, and psychomotor. It is intellectual, attitudinal, behavioral.

Chandos Reid Rice (1974) said that the supervisor working with curriculum change needs to have a belief in the worth of each individual; a belief in the use of intelligence, problem solving, and decision making; a belief that every individual has the right to participate in decisions that affect him or her.

Surely, this is characteristic of self-directedness. Whatever plan is used to develop or expand programs for self-directed learning should encourage use of these characteristics of self-direction.

In summary, these factors must be considered in planning or implementing programs for self-directed learning:

1. The school environment, its culture and the values it emphasizes;

2. The leadership role of the administrator in (a) exhibiting the characteristics of self-directedness, of self-actualization, or the helping

professional, and in (b) facilitating and supporting these characteristics in others;

3. The processes of the curriculum change model in encouraging and supporting self-directed learning.

As Goodlad (1975, p. 110) commented: "The single school is the largest and the proper unit for educational change."

A Parable

Once there was a class
investigating vibrations.
Every day they studied a special vibration.
The first day they studied vibrations in
sound.
The second day they studied vibrations
in objects.
The third day they studied vibrations
in their bodies.
The fourth day they enjoyed the vibrations
of the room.
The fifth day was the best;
they took a walk
around their school
and felt all the vibrations
of all the people.

Jon Rye Kinghorn (1978, p. 56)

References

Barbara Biber and Patricia Minuchin. "The Impact of School Philosophy and Practice on Child Development." In: Norman V. Overly, editor. *The Unstudied Curriculum: Its Impact on Children.* Washington, D.C.: Association for Supervision and Curriculum Development, 1970.

Lois Jerry Blanchard. "The Values of the School: A Study of Student and Staff Perceptions of the Goals of the School and the Hidden Curriculum." Unpublished doctoral dissertation, Wayne State University, 1977.

Arthur Combs *et al. Florida Studies in the Helping Professions.* Gainesville: University of Florida Press, 1969.

Arthur Combs, Donald L. Avila, and William K. Purkey. *Helping Relationships: Basic Concepts for the Helping Professions.* Boston: Allyn and Bacon, Inc., 1971.

Richard B. Copeland. "The Relationship of Effective Building Administrators and Their Perceptual Organization." Unpublished doctoral dissertation, Wayne State University, 1976.

John Goodlad. "Schools Can Make a Difference." *Educational Leadership.* 33(2)108-17; November 1975.

Jon Rye Kinghorn. "A Parable." *NASSP Bulletin* 62(420); October 1978.

James B. Macdonald. "The Quality of Everyday Life in School." In: James B. Macdonald and Esther Zaret, editors. *Schools in Search of Meaning.* Washington, D.C.: Association for Supervision and Curriculum Development, 1975.

Patricia Minuchin *et al. The Psychological Impact of School Experience: A Comparative Study of Nine-Year Old Children in Contrasting Schools.* New York: Basic Books, Inc., 1969.

Chandos Reid Rice. "Looking Into the Future Out of the Past." Address presented to the Annual Conference of the Association for Supervision and Curriculum Development, Anaheim, California, March 1974.

J. Lloyd Trump and William Georgiades. *How to Change Your School.* Reston, Virginia: National Association of Secondary School Principals, 1978.

Elizabeth Vallance. "Hiding the Hidden Curriculum: An Interpretation of the Language of Justification in Nineteenth Century Educational Reform." *Curriculum Theory Network* 4(1); 1973-74.

"Waterford Model for Instructional Planning." Unpublished paper. Waterford, Michigan: Waterford School District, 1976.

Contributors

JAMES J. BERRY, Professor of Psychology, Oakland Community College, Farmington, Michigan

LOIS JERRY BLANCHARD, Director of Secondary Education, Waterford School District, Waterford, Michigan

ARTHUR L. COSTA, Chairman, Department of Educational Administration, California State University, Sacramento, California

DELMO DELLA-DORA, Professor, Department of Teacher Education, California State University/Hayward, Hayward, California

BENJAMIN P. EBERSOLE, Assistant Superintendent for Curriculum, Baltimore County Schools, Towson, Maryland.

MARIO D. FANTINI, Dean, School of Education, University of Massachusetts, Amherst, Massachusetts

RICHARD L. FOSTER, Consultant, Greenbrae, California

ANTHONY F. GREGORC, Associate Professor, Department of Secondary Education, The University of Connecticut, Storrs, Connecticut

CLAIRE HALVERSON, Assistant Professor, University of Wisconsin-Extension, Center for Urban Community Development, Milwaukee, Wisconsin

PAT KNUDSEN, Principal, Crescent Lake School, Waterford School District, Waterford, Michigan

ALBERTO M. OCHOA, Director, National Origin Desegregation Center and Assistant Professor, Multicultural Education Department, San Diego State University, San Diego, California

JAMES V. ORR, Professor of English, Oakland Community College, Farmington, Michigan

ANA MARIA RODRIGUEZ, Assistant Professor, Multicultural Education Department, San Diego State University, San Diego, California

BARBARA A. SIZEMORE, Associate Professor, Department of Black Community Education Research and Development, University of Pittsburgh, Pittsburgh, Pennsylvania

NANCY M. SPENCER, Training Coordinator, Hampshire Educational Collaborative Title IV-C Development Center, Amherst, Massachusetts

JAMES D.WELLS, Associate Professor of Education, Florida International University, Miami, Florida

EDWIN P. WHITE, Supervisor of Science Education, Virginia Department of Education, Richmond, Virginia

Acknowledgments

Publication of this booklet was the responsibility of Ron Brandt, Executive Editor, ASCD publications. Nancy Olson provided editing and production services with the assistance of Elsa Angell, Patsy Connors, Anne Dees, and Gwendolyn Spells.

ASCD Publications, Summer 1979

Yearbooks

Education for an Open Society
(610-74012) $8.00
Education for Peace: Focus on Mankind
(610-17946) $7.50
Evaluation as Feedback and Guide
(610-17700) $6.50
Feeling, Valuing, and the Art of Growing:
Insights into the Affective
(610-77104) $9.75
Freedom, Bureaucracy, & Schooling
(610-17508) $6.50
Improving the Human Condition: A Curricular
Response to Critical Realities
(610-78132) $9.75
Learning and Mental Health in the School
(610-17674) $5.00
Life Skills in School and Society
(610-17786) $5.50
Lifelong Learning—A Human Agenda
(610-79160) $9.75
A New Look at Progressive Education
(610-17812) $8.00
Perspectives on Curriculum Development
1776-1976 (610-76078) $9.50
Schools in Search of Meaning
(610-75044) $8.50
Perceiving, Behaving, Becoming: A New Focus
for Education (610-17278) $5.00
To Nurture Humaneness: Commitment for
the '70's (610-17810) $6.00

Books and Booklets

About Learning Materials (611-78134) $4.50
Action Learning: Student Community Service
Projects (611-74018) $2.50
Adventuring, Mastering, Associating: New
Strategies for Teaching Children
(611-76080) $5.00
Beyond Jencks: The Myth of Equal Schooling
(611-17928) $2.00
Bilingual Education for Latinos
(611-78142) $6.75
The Changing Curriculum: Mathematics
(611-17724) $2.00
Classroom-Relevant Research in the Language
Arts (611-78140) $7.50
Criteria for Theories of Instruction
(611-17756) $2.00
Curricular Concerns in a Revolutionary Era
(611-17852) $6.00
Curriculum Leaders: Improving Their Influence
(611-76084) $4.00
Curriculum Theory (611-77112) $7.00
Degrading the Grading Myths: A Primer of
Alternatives to Grades and Marks
(611-76082) $6.00
Differentiated Staffing (611-17924) $3.50
Discipline for Today's Children and Youth
(611-17314) $1.50
Educational Accountability: Beyond Behavioral
Objectives (611-17856) $2.50
Elementary School Mathematics: A Guide to
Current Research (611-75056) $5.00
Elementary School Science: A Guide to
Current Research (611-17726) $2.25
Eliminating Ethnic Bias in Instructional
Materials: Comment and Bibliography
(611-74020) $3.25
Emerging Moral Dimensions in Society:
Implications for Schooling
(611-75052) $3.75
Ethnic Modification of the Curriculum
(611-17832) $1.00
Global Studies: Problems and Promises for
Elementary Teachers (611-76086) $4.50
Humanistic Education: Objectives and
Assessment (611-78136) $4.75
The Humanities and the Curriculum
(611-17708) $2.00

Impact of Decentralization on Curriculum:
Selected Viewpoints (611-75050) $3.75
Improving Educational Assessment & An
Inventory of Measures of Affective
Behavior (611-17804) $4.50
International Dimension of Education
(611-17816) $2.25
Interpreting Language Arts Research for the
Teacher (611-17846) $4.00
Learning More About Learning
(611-17310) $2.00
Linguistics and the Classroom Teacher
(611-17720) $2.75
A Man for Tomorrow's World
(611-17838) $2.25
Middle School in the Making
(611-74024) $5.00
The Middle School We Need
(611-75060) $2.50
Moving Toward Self-Directed Learning
(611-79166) $4.75
Multicultural Education: Commitments, Issues,
and Applications (611-77108) $7.00
Needs Assessment: A Focus for Curriculum
Development (611-75048) $4.00
Observational Methods in the Classroom
(611-17948) $3.50
Open Education: Critique and Assessment
(611-75054) $4.75
Professional Supervision for Professional
Teachers (611-75046) $4.50
Removing Barriers to Humaneness in the High
School (611-17848) $2.50
Reschooling Society: A Conceptual Model
(611-17950) $2.00
The School of the Future—NOW
(611-17920) $3.75
Schools Become Accountable: A PACT
Approach (611-74016) $3.50
The School's Role as Moral Authority
(611-77110) $4.50
Selecting Learning Experiences: Linking
Theory and Practice (611-78138) $4.75
Social Studies for the Evolving Individual
(611-17952) $3.00
Staff Development: Staff Liberation
(611-77106) $6.50
Supervision: Emerging Profession
(611-17796) $5.00
Supervision in a New Key (611-17926) $2.50
Supervision: Perspectives and Propositions
(611-17732) $2.00
What Are the Sources of the Curriculum?
(611-17522) $1.50
Vitalizing the High School (611-74026) $3.50
Developmental Characteristics of Children and
Youth (wall chart) (611-75058) $2.00

Discounts on quantity orders of same title to
single address: 10-49 copies, 10%; 50 or more
copies, 15%. Make checks or money orders
payable to ASCD. Orders totaling $10.00 or
less must be prepaid. Orders from institutions
and businesses must be on official purchase
order form. Shipping and handling charges will
be added to billed purchase orders. *Please be
sure to list the stock number of each publication, shown in parentheses.*

Subscription to *Educational Leadership*—$15.00
a year. ASCD Membership dues: Regular (subscription [$15] and yearbook)—$25.00 a year;
Comprehensive (includes subscription [$15]
and yearbook plus other books and booklets
distributed during period of membership)—
$35.00 a year.

Order from:
Association for Supervision and
Curriculum Development
225 North Washington Street
Alexandria, Virginia 22314